Sharing Faith
the Jesus Way

Jim Currin

Text copyright © Jim Currin 2011
The author asserts the moral right
to be identified as the author of this work

Published by
The Bible Reading Fellowship
15 The Chambers, Vineyard
Abingdon OX14 3FE
United Kingdom
Tel: +44 (0)1865 319700
Email: enquiries@brf.org.uk
Website: www.brf.org.uk
BRF is a Registered Charity

ISBN 978 1 84101 862 1
First published 2011
10 9 8 7 6 5 4 3 2 1 0
All rights reserved

Acknowledgments

Unless otherwise stated, scripture quotations are taken from the Holy Bible, New International
Version, copyright © 1973, 1978, 1984 by International Bible Society, and are used by
permission of Hodder & Stoughton Publishers, a member of the Hachette Livre UK Group.
All rights reserved. 'NIV' is a registered trademark of International Bible Society. UK trademark
number 1448790.

Scripture quotations taken from The New Revised Stand Version of the Bible, Anglicised
Edition, copyright © 1989, 1995 by the Division of Christian Education of the National
Council of the Churches of Christ in the United States of America, are used by permission.
All rights reserved.

A catalogue record for this book is available from the British Library

Printed in Singapore by Craft Print International Ltd

Sharing Faith
the Jesus Way

Jim Currin

Acknowledgments

Thank you to colleagues and friends, especially David Spriggs, Robin Trew, Debbie Brown, Kate Lucas and All Saints, Allesley. This book is dedicated to Linda, without whom it could not have been written.

Contents

Foreword

You are unique. There has never been anyone quite like you. Your genes are different from anyone else's. The remarkable truth about God is that God relates to each of us as individuals. The psalmist expressed that truth in poetry: 'You... formed my inward parts; you knit me together in my mother's womb' (Psalm 139:13, NRSV).

This wise and generous exploration of evangelism begins with that truth, exploring how Jesus responded differently to individuals according to their needs and the state of their lives. Good evangelism begins there, respecting our own individuality as we share the faith that shapes us and respecting our conversation partner, too.

In days gone by, people in Western Europe learnt the biblical story from clergy, teachers and parents. Now, for the first time in about 1500 years, ordinary Christians need to be missionaries to people of their own culture who have no background knowledge of the faith. That is a daunting task, and one for which we are largely unprepared. This delightful little book will be a source of courage for those of us who don't quite know where to begin—and, for those who have begun the journey, it is a compendium of wisdom, humour and ideas.

Use it, and let the 360 degree gospel of Jesus surprise and entrance you.

The Revd Dr David Cornick
General Secretary of Churches Together in England

Introduction

Jesus often took people by surprise. He did so in the Gospels and he does so today.

I hope you will be surprised as you read *Sharing Faith the Jesus Way*. Surprised because of what Jesus did 2000 years ago and surprised because of what he does today. I pray that the biggest surprise will be what he does through you.

Together we shall explore the principles that I trust will make it possible, natural and a positive experience to share your faith—positive both for you and for the people you meet. It would be great if you felt like Tracy, who said, 'I am not ashamed to say I believe in Jesus; I just don't want it to sound corny.'

Sharing faith is personal but it is not private. It is doubtful that we would be Christians today if the disciples of Jesus had not told others in their day. We are links in a 2000-year-old chain. So how are we to pass on the good news of Jesus Christ? I believe the key is to see how Jesus did it himself.

It is tempting to think that the main way the good news spread was through the preaching of Peter, Paul and the great preachers who have followed them. Patrick in Ireland and Augustine in England are examples of those who helped to bring the gospel to British shores. We can be inspired that an estimated three million people worldwide have responded to Billy Graham's invitation to follow Christ. However, we should also appreciate that the gospel travelled down the centuries in a wide variety of ways. Chiefly it was through ordinary Christians doing ordinary things made extraordinary by the Holy Spirit—and this is where you and I come in.

'I don't mind sharing my faith,' said Debbie, 'but I don't do evangelism.' Well, that was a surprise to me for several reasons. One, I knew that Debbie had been on mission teams overseas several times. Two, she is a natural evangelist and happily talks to all sorts of people about Jesus. Three, sharing faith is evangelism. 'Yes, it is,' she said, 'but I don't like all the negative stuff that goes with it!'

Is there a way forward that avoids 'the negative stuff'? The answer is a resounding 'Yes!' and I believe that Jesus shows the way. In the first chapter of this book, we will look at good and bad practice, and see that much of the 'negative stuff' is a distortion of the way in which Jesus did evangelism himself.

The 'Jesus way'

First let's consider a quotation that I think illustrates the 'Jesus way' well:

An essentially biblical emphasis—all too often ignored by the church—is that Christ is Lord and Saviour of the whole of a person, or he is no saviour at all. Because Jesus insisted on seeing the person whole, one could never be sure which aspect of a person's need he would tackle first. Here comes the paralysed man, helpless and obviously sick in body. His friends have bought him hoping for a simple cure, and Jesus talks about the forgiveness of sins. Here on the other hand comes a clear case of spiritual need, an enquirer asking how to gain eternal life, and Jesus gives him an economic answer, telling him how to give away his goods to the poor. Because ultimately Jesus cannot rest content until all of a [person's] needs are fully met, it does not matter much to him where he starts on the work of salvation.[1]

This quote gives a big picture of the gospel message. That message points in all directions. It addresses a variety of situations. It is not narrow but all-encompassing: I like to think of it as the '360' gospel of Jesus.

With this in mind, we'll look at the Jesus way of sharing faith. I say 'we', as I see this as an adventure that we shall go on together.

I hope you will pray about the 'Jesus way', try some of the exercises at the end of each section and see how they apply in practice with the people you know. I also hope that you will discuss with others in your church or study group. The book will provide some resources to help with that, so that we can encourage each other in this privileged task.

Some questions you might have

Should we share our faith at all? You may think it is difficult, questionable and even objectionable to do so. John is a friend who put it this way: 'I think it's offensive to try to convert someone to my religion, so I don't do it.' At the same time, you may be familiar with the parable of the lost sheep—how the shepherd left the 99 that were safe and went after the one that was lost (Luke 15:1–7), and you may know the words of Jesus' great commission: 'Go and make disciples of all nations' (Matthew 28:19). Perhaps you have been frequently reminded that this commission applies as much to you as it does to anyone else!

'Sharing faith' is a dilemma that faces many Christians on a daily basis. It's a tension we feel with friends, family, neighbours and colleagues—in fact, probably, with everyone we meet. On the one hand, we don't want to be a 'Bible basher' and put people off, while on the other hand some of us feel empty or dry in our faith and think we have nothing meaningful to say. We either feel guilty because we have failed to talk about our faith or relieved that we have remained anonymous. Be assured, I am not going to describe lots of success stories and leave you discouraged because they don't reflect your experience. Rather, I hope to encourage you with stories of everyday faith journeys, illustrating the general principles that we see in the Gospels and in the lives of the rich variety of people within our churches. To help us, we will look at findings from the *Faith Journeys*[2] website provided by Christian Research,[3] with which I work closely.

Another issue that you may be thinking about is the difference between words and actions. I say this because people often say, 'Actions speak louder than words', implying that we don't have to say anything at all. I think that both are fundamental to the Jesus way and we do both a disservice if we separate them. Indeed, people often come to faith in Christ today by experiencing Christianity in a group or church without any explanation of the gospel: it is only later that they come to know what they believe. It may be then that we will have something to say to them. We should be prepared.

There are plenty of people who may be interested in Jesus, just like this young woman brought up in a Hindu home:

As I grew up, I was interested in all religions. And then I started thinking about Jesus. A school friend was a Christian and I read various books. These led me to make a prayer of commitment just before a piano lesson. I went to the piano teacher and said, 'I have just become a Christian.' I was captivated by Jesus. He was not an establishment figure. He was not dictated to by anyone. I liked the way he related to people and I thought the Sermon on the Mount was brilliantly intelligent. He was not afraid of whether he lived or died for what he believed. He was passionate but not compromised by himself or his morals. I was, as I say, captivated by Jesus.

So how do people find out about Jesus? There are myriad different ways, and no one way is more important than another. The only really important thing is that people find faith and become disciples.

St Francis is often quoted as saying, 'Go into the world and preach the gospel: use words if you have to.' Commenting on this quote, the Dominican friar Timothy Radcliffe said, 'Actually, when we look at Jesus we also see that he said a lot.'[4] To deepen any relationship, we eventually need to say something! The question is more about what, how and when. Christians often find it harder to 'say' than to 'do'—which is one reason why I want to explore 'saying' in these pages. Jesus used words, and so should we.

You may be thinking, 'No one's interested.' Michael is a friend who recently said, 'Most books on evangelism start with the assumption that people are interested in finding out about the Christian faith—but not many people are interested!' I understand the comment, and the one made by another friend who said, 'Many of us go about our day-to-day lives without ever coming across someone wanting an explanation of the gospel.' I want to make it possible for you to be prepared when someone is interested, and to have the confidence to start a conversation when the right opportunity arises. How many more people could be captivated by Jesus if we knew how to share our faith?

We are not Jesus. The miracles we perform are not very dramatic. We are not the bread of life and we do not have the authority to forgive sins. People would travel the world to meet us if we changed water into wine but they don't even ask about coming to church. While this is true, they are probably still interested in spiritual things, as research in Kendal, UK, has shown.[5] The big questions of life do not go away. There are plenty of natural points of contact that can make sharing our faith not only possible but also a fruitful experience for you and the other person. You may be a new Christian yourself and know this to be true.

Have you found it easy to share your faith? If so, how?

Whether I'm taking someone sailing or out on a motorbike pillion ride, I love to introduce people to a new experience. It is a fantastic joy to open up a new world for them, especially if it then becomes more than just a good memory and they develop an interest that lasts for life. For the Christian, the greatest privilege and joy is to introduce someone to Jesus. This task has been called evangelism, the sharing of the 'good news', or 'gospel'. I want to explore this, not in the way in which many of us have come to think of evangelism but in the way Jesus did it.

People today

People today don't like to be preached at. They don't like to be told what to do, especially by 'religious people'. We can't even assume that they are interested if we have a good story to tell. They may avoid us if they feel that we are likely to be intrusive.

Even so, 72 per cent of the population said (for whatever reason) that they were 'Christian' in the 2001 census. In the UK, 1.3 million people have already completed an Alpha course and 7.4 million know that the course is about Christianity. Each year, 78 per cent of people visit a church as tourists and 'recent research has shown that even those who are openly hostile to the Church and "Christians" in the abstract have a high opinion of Jesus and commonly speak positively of real Christians, whom they actually know'.[6]

People like to think of themselves as following their own spiritual path, and they don't mind where they pick up things that help them. As Christians, we might have lots of questions about this tendency but we need to start where these people are. This is precisely the approach that Jesus took in addressing spiritual need 2000 years ago. It is part of the Jesus way that we should explore today.

It would be great if you were to note questions as you go along and then discuss what you are reading with a friend or study group.

In these pages I hope that you will:

- read the Bible, and especially some of the Gospels, afresh.
- gain confidence in your own Christian life.
- understand the process of sharing faith.
- find some solutions to the complexity of life and faith.
- witness transformation in the lives of other people as they find new life in Christ.
- 'return with great joy' like the first disciples who were sent out by Jesus (Luke 10:1–17).

I won't be expecting you to decide to go abroad as a missionary or undertake a particular project (although who knows where the journey may lead you?). Indeed, you probably will not end up doing lots of extra things in addition to what you would normally do. The heart of faith-sharing is about being available, as Jesus and the disciples were, to discover what God is going to do next with you and the people you meet.

Witnessing and evangelism

Just like people who have seen a crime being committed or attended a marriage ceremony, we are witnesses to the events and stories that we experience. If you go to church, pray and read about Jesus in the Gospels, you are witnesses to these things, too. If we share our faith, we are also doing evangelism. Now, some people are called to the specific role of an 'evangelist', so what is the difference? It is simply that 'evangelists' undertake projects or activities on purpose to make an opportunity to share their faith. They are also called to equip the whole church to be doing evangelism as well (Ephesians 4:11–13).

As we are looking at the 'Jesus way', it is important to note that the words 'evangelism' and 'evangelist' are not to be found in the four written Gospels. The Church has called the Gospel writers the 'four Evangelists' but the term is not used for Jesus or his disciples. However, my view is that when Jesus called the fishermen to follow him and, in the same breath, said that he would make them fishers of men (Matthew 4:19), what they went on to do is what we now call 'evangelism'.

So, you may not be called to be an evangelist, but you are called to evangelism. Whether we like it or not, we are witnesses to our faith. The question is, 'How well do we do it?'

It is important to remember that we are not asked to do evangelism simply by using our own gifts and abilities, but by using the insights and power of the Holy Spirit, who helps us put the principles into practice. He often prompts us and provides the situation and the way forward in it. I have often heard it said that 'success in witnessing is simply presenting Jesus Christ, in the power of the Holy Spirit, and leaving the results to God'.

It's not what you say but what they hear that matters

We talk to people every day. More precisely, we talk and listen—because we know that if we do all the talking, people soon lose interest. We see this in the Gospels, where Jesus is recorded as having many one-to-one conversations with the people he met. He would often ask a question, make a comment and then ask another question. One well-known passage in the Bible that records one such conversation has a very strange twist at the end. It is known as 'Peter's confession of Christ'. Read Matthew 16:13–20 and think about what the twist might be and why Jesus said it.

Jesus' way was not to preach at people so much as to engage in a dialogue. This is illustrated in the most basic picture of the two-way communication between two people:

You ⇄ A.N. Other

Effective two-way communication leads to building a common understanding and a good relationship. This is the key to Jesus' way and we see it demonstrated chiefly in the relationship between Jesus and his first followers. We shall also see it in his brief encounters with people he met along the way in everyday situations: for example, the woman at the well, the paralysed man who was let down through the roof, the rich young ruler, the teacher of the law, the centurion, Zacchaeus and Nicodemus. In many of these encounters, we see words, actions and non-verbal communication, such as a healing, miracle or some other experience that made the good news clear.

The simple diagram opposite is a model of how we should share our faith in Jesus today. We should not preach at people, but neither should we stay silent. We should develop a dialogue, even if it is short. While some people have heard Jesus speak to them in a dream, or committed their life to Christ after reading about him in a hotel Gideon Bible, remember that most will hear about him in conversation through 'ordinary Christians' like you and me.

The art of connecting three stories

Sharing our Christian faith today involves three stories. There is your story, there is the story of the other person, and there is God's story in Jesus. The interaction between these stories forms a 'triangle of relationships'. How do you share faith the Jesus way? The brief answer is to develop a three-way relationship between you, the other person and God. In practice, this relationship will be different in every situation.

As we shall see, in the Jesus way there is no 'set piece', pattern or formula to follow. The nearest we get to such a thing is Jesus' invitation to 'follow me'. Jesus had a different approach to each person he met—and so shall we. Your story, their story and God's story all exist anyway; the art is to connect them together. You will become better able to do that by being more familiar with God's story in the Bible, your own story as you reflect on your faith journey, and the other person's story as you have conversations and build a relationship with them. The Holy Spirit will show us the way as we pray for the people we know and meet.

Here is an expanded view of what happens when we share our faith, with God at the top of the triangle, you on the left and the other person on the right. Read the next paragraph slowly to see what relationships the arrows represent.

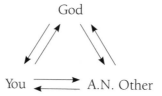

God's love for you (left arrow down) and your love for him (left arrow up) are ongoing. Your relationship with the other person (bottom arrow right and left) is growing. God also loves the other person (right arrow down). Our hope and prayer are that the other person will respond and love God too (right arrow up). As we explore the principles behind this diagram in the following chapters, my prayer is that you will see how this works out in practice. Every time Jesus encountered people, it was different. It will be for you, too.

The need for us all to share our faith is great. Not only do we have the transforming message of God's love, forgiveness and new life in Christ, but we have hope for the world. It is very exciting and there are lots of stories of how hope is being brought to people today. People are being healed, relationships are being restored and communities are being built. It is a herald and foretaste of God's kingdom 'on earth as it is in heaven' as people respond to God's love for them. This is illustrated by June, who tells her story briefly below. Her story is more dramatic than many, but it shows what a difference sharing your faith can make to someone else. It also shows how powerfully the gospel can work in someone's life:

I was encouraged to attend Sunday school, and then, as a teenager, broke away for a while. I gave my life to Jesus after I was healed of agoraphobia. I received the laying on of hands and went down on the floor 'in the Spirit'. The next day, after having been confined to the house for six months, I got on the bus and went into town. I thought, 'If Jesus can heal me like this, then I will work for him.'

Tailor-made gospel

Jesus' model is not 'one size fits all'. Just like in the facets of a diamond, what you see depends on the angle from which you're looking. Let's consider some of the various things Jesus said to people as he spoke to their personal situations:

- 'Repent and believe.'
- 'Follow me.'
- 'Give away your goods to the poor.'
- 'He who endures to the end will be saved.'
- 'Take up your cross.'
- 'You must be born again.'
- 'Blessed are the pure in heart, for they shall see God.'

There are many more things that Jesus said to would-be followers. His statements may even seem contradictory, but they all fit together as part of the gospel message. In Appendix A you find a list of 'Top 50 texts for the 360 gospel of Jesus'—and this is still not the full list of things Jesus said about eternal life, as I originally counted 84 of them!

The big picture of the Jesus way is illustrated by two different men who asked Jesus the same question: 'What must I do to inherit eternal life?' (Mark 10:17–21 and Luke 10:25–28). Interestingly, Jesus gave them different answers. This surprises some Christians, who assume they should give the impression that Jesus said the same thing to everyone he met. The preacher whose message is always 'You must be born again' (which is what Jesus said to Nicodemus: see John 3:3) is one example. In the Jesus way, we see that many different things can be said when we are explaining the gospel. Not surprisingly, as we look at the stories of faith journeys today, we also see that we have all responded in different ways to the call of Christ. There is a facet of the gospel that speaks to everyone individually. The gospel is tailor-made.

So we'll start as Jesus does with you—as you are, at the moment.

A note on the Gospels

Just a note about how I have approached the four books that we call Gospels. I have taken them as read, just as the text has been given to us. I appreciate the extensive ways of studying, like the 'historical-critical' method, and all the different questions about interpretation (called 'hermeneutics', if you want to search on the internet). However, like many Christian writers today,[7] I feel that these can get in the way of a fresh look at Jesus and his way, so this book will take a straight reading of the Gospel texts.

I write a lot more about this in *The 360 Gospel of Jesus* (Grove Books, 2011) and on the website www.jesus360.org. uk.

Chapter 1

Jesus accepts you as you are

'You are a Jew and I am a Samaritan woman. How can you ask me for a drink?'
JOHN 4:9

....

Almost equal proportions first considered themselves a Christian during pre-teen (34%), teen (33%) and adult years (33%).
CHRISTIAN RESEARCH

....

Jesus surprised many people. Take the Samaritan woman at the well, whose story is told in John 4. Here Jesus speaks (a) to a woman, (b) to a Samaritan, and (c) to an outcast (because she had had five husbands). Not only does he acknowledge her presence but he even dares to look at her, and then, amazingly, speaks to her. Even more extraordinary for his day, he does not take the expected moral high ground but simply asks for water. This is a gentle gesture of acceptance that shouts, 'RADICAL!'

Read John 4:4–42 for the full account of this powerful story.

Without an ounce of judgment or a single pronouncement, Jesus embarks on a deep theological discussion in the heat of the day with a woman he doesn't know, and, in a few short sentences, transforms her life. The result is that 'many of the Samaritans from that town believed in him because of the woman's testimony' (v. 39). This astonishing outcome was predicated on Jesus accepting the woman as she was, not the way other people might have liked her to be. She was transformed and then spontaneously shared her experience with her community.

Because Jesus accepts you as you are, you too can relax when it comes to sharing your faith. You don't have to be perfect. You don't need specialist knowledge or to be well trained. You don't have to be particularly gifted or have a dramatic story of conversion to tell, like June's in the Introduction. You just have to be yourself, knowing that God loves and accepts you. Probably the only qualification you need is a desire to know more of God in Christ. Like the woman at the well, you need to want to come close to Jesus and take in everything he has to offer. Then, as you look to Jesus, God can use you, regardless of who you are and what you have done.

This is a very important point, as many Christians seem to think they have to be like someone else. Of course, famous Christians such as John Wesley, C.S. Lewis and Mother Teresa had great gifts, but, in God's economy, so have you. Don't forget that!

So, let's start where you are with your own experience of faith. In this chapter, we will aim to explore:

- Our own faith journeys
- Good and bad experiences of evangelism
- How personality shapes the way we share faith

Our own faith journeys

'Sir, give me this water.'
JOHN 4:15

35 per cent were first aware of being a Christian as a result of a sudden experience, but for 64 per cent it was more gradual.
CHRISTIAN RESEARCH

I am assuming that if you are reading this book, you want to find out more about your Christian faith and how you can share it with other people. That seems an obvious thing to say, but it does gloss over a lot of questions. Where are you with God at the moment? Do you feel that you have something to share?

As we have seen already, Jesus accepts us as we are. You may have had an amazing Christian experience and can't wait to tell everyone about it. Thank God if you have. Alternatively, you may be feeling far from God and wondering if faith is just a delusion. If you are, simply accept it as the way you are for the time being.

Many of us are probably somewhere between these two positions, or perhaps on a gentle rollercoaster ride that goes up and down between the two on a daily basis. It doesn't matter if one day your Christian faith means a lot to you and another day it doesn't. After all, Jesus did his very greatest work after crying out, 'My God, why have you forsaken me?' (Mark 15:34). God uses us when we trust him; we don't have to feel good and close to God.

Take a few moments to think about yourself and your relationship with God as it is at the moment. Be honest. Try to describe it in a single word or sentence, perhaps writing it down somewhere private. Pray quietly for a while and thank God for the faith you have. Remember that one way in which Jesus discovered his identity was through his temptations in the wilderness (Matthew 4:1–11). Your relationship with God may be strengthened as you work through difficulties, too.

On the *Faith Journeys* website, we're told that while 33 per cent of people became a Christian after a sudden experience, for 66 per cent the experience was more gradual. Like any journey, there are ups and downs, twists and turns, and times of encouragement in the Christian life. Often, these events are small but sometimes they can be noted like stepping stones along the way. Think of your own faith journey. Start to think of these stepping stone experiences, however big or small they are. Write them down as you remember them and then number them in chronological order.

It can be helpful to draw a timeline of these experiences, to map out your faith journey. To do this, use a new sheet of plain A4 paper and draw a line across the middle. This is your timeline, and 'now' is on the far right-hand side. Think how far back your journey goes and therefore how long a time the line represents: it might be two years or several decades.

On the paper, write down the numbers from your list of experiences at the points corresponding with how far back in time they occurred. Each experience may have been good or bad, so indicate this by putting the number above or below the middle line. If it was a really bad experience a long time ago, for example, your number will be to the left of the page near the bottom.

When you have finished plotting your experiences, your timeline might look something like this.

		4 3 2			9 10
			6	8	Now
		5	7		
1					

When I suggest doing this experience in groups, half of those present say, 'This doesn't work for me', while the other half are excited and find the process illuminating. Don't worry if you are in the former group! At the end of this section, you will find alternative ways to illustrate your story creatively.

We often see God working in our lives in retrospect or when we hear of other people's experiences. When we compare notes, we immediately see how different our stories are.

Here is mine, which you have seen illustrated on the timeline above, with each vertical line representing ten years.

1 Going to church and Sunday School as a child.
2 Learning to ring church bells with other youngsters, including girls!
3 Serving at the altar and hearing the call to follow Jesus, especially in the hymn lines: 'In simple trust like theirs who heard, beside the Syrian Sea, the gracious calling of the Lord, let us, like them, without a word, rise up and follow thee' (John Whittier, 1872).
4 A Larry Norman gospel concert, with enthusiastic young people shouting, 'Give us a J. Give us an E. Give us an S. Give us a U. Give us another S. What have you got? JESUS!' and the crystal-clear words of the song 'I wish we'd all been ready'. That night I prayed my own prayer of commitment.
5 My three-year theological training. I loved being in the Church Army but found the biblical criticism which was popular at the time quite destructive to my faith.
6 Commissioned as a Church Army evangelist and sent out on missions—seeing people become Christians.
7 My own version of what St John of the Cross called 'the dark night of the soul'.
8, 9 and 10 Various highlights in recent years. I am thankful that, on balance, life is very good, God feels close, issues get resolved, prayer feels meaningful and church is a positive place to be.

The fact that we all have different faith journeys is one of the key aspects of the Jesus way. As we respond to Jesus in different ways, so the people we seek to reach will respond in different ways, too. This is very exciting and opens all kinds of doors, but is a great challenge to the traditional way in which some people have sometimes 'preached the gospel' in the past.

Follow-up activities

As promised, here are two other ways of representing your faith journey. Think and pray about what you produce.

- **Alternative 1**: Imagine yourself on a long walk, going up and down a path. Take a piece of paper and draw the 'valleys and mountain-top experiences' as a simple line, showing the ups and downs of your spiritual journey. Include any features—for example, where the journey starts, a line break, plateau, valley, storm, wall, rainbow, and so on. Be creative and note down some details of any significant moments in your life and faith journey along the way.
- **Alternative 2**: Imagine you are looking down on to a map. Take a piece of paper to represent this map and think of your faith journey while you draw a path as the main feature. It might meander, go between rocks, become a short motorway, or come to roadworks! Draw each feature along the way, which might vary in width, colour, texture or shape, as well as direction. The path may go back on itself or just peter out in a desert. Add various

weather features that illustrate what was happening at different times—for example, storm clouds and thunder, or bright sunshine. You could even depict different forms of transport along the route, from bus to balloon, if that is relevant and helpful.

Next, have a look on the *Faith Journeys* website and consider writing up your faith journey for other people to read. By adding your story, you will be contributing to a relatively new nationwide online research project and helping the wider church to get a bigger picture about how people come to faith. For example, one survey of 207 people provided some of the information quoted in this chapter. We shall consider more findings near the end of Chapter 4.

Meet up with a friend and say that you are reading this book. Pray together. Share the main points that you remember from what you have read and talk about whether or not they echo your own experience. Talk together about any picture of your faith journey you have drawn. Better still, suggest to your friend that you both do one of the follow-up activities above, and compare notes afterwards.

Good and bad experiences of evangelism

Unfortunately, there are plenty of bad examples of the ways in which people have tried to share their faith. You probably have some stories to share—as I do. My hunch is that many of these bad examples could not be described as the 'Jesus way'.

Sadly, the history of the Church includes accounts of coercion, manipulation, politics and brute force, all of which have been used to make people 'Christian'. A study of this subject is beyond our scope here, but it is sufficient to say that both the Church and individual Christians need to repent of the way they have treated others, even if they had the best of intentions.

If you have had a bad experience at the hands of Christians, I am sorry—not least because this will be one of the reasons why I suspect many of you find it difficult to share your faith today. A summary of what I have heard many people say is, 'I don't want to be like them—Bible-bashing, pushy, and uninterested in me personally.' Some of you may even have experienced behaviour so abusive that it calls for a healing process, including specialist help.

I have to say that my own experience of discovering faith in Christ, and of passing it on to others as a newly committed Christian, turned out to be an exciting and life-changing adventure. Interestingly, though, it was soon followed by a bad experience.

I'll share the good experience first: number 4 on my time-line, which occurred 40 years ago but is still crystal clear in my mind. After the Larry Norman concert and my personal prayer of commitment in the middle of the night, I could not stop talking about Jesus. I was about 15 years old at the time and found myself being picked on by someone at school. During morning break, I was cornered next to the boys' toilets with the question, 'If Jesus comes again, will it be on a motorbike?' That was the most polite of all the questions the other boy went on to ask me! A large crowd quickly gathered, thinking there was going to be a fight. I prayed for God's help and answered as best I could. Remarkably, after some time, my assailant pronounced, 'Well, I think Jesus was just a good miracle man!'

I was overcome with emotion—relief that I wasn't being beaten up but, at the same time, exhilaration that I was making him defend his own view of Jesus. I thought, 'This is where Jesus would be, not hanging around in the church but out here in the playground.' It was then that I felt called to work with 'people outside the church', which eventually led to me finding out about, and joining, the Church Army.

Now here is the bad experience. I hadn't a clue that 'working with people outside the church' was 'evangelism'. To find out more, I volunteered for a mission training weekend in a nearby town. I wanted to learn as much as I could, but it felt awkward. The programme and training revolved around open-air preaching and giving out leaflets. We were also sent out to do some door-knocking and were trained in what to say—which included inviting people to hear a preacher whom I did not really like myself! It all felt a bit forced. Perhaps it was something about the people in that particular town, but I was not surprised when very few of them seemed interested in what we were trying to do. It just didn't seem to fit.

By contrast, here is another story from a few years later, when I was a student. Five of us shared a house, and three of us were Christians and good friends with each other. We prayed together and felt concerned that, because we were in the 'majority', it would be unfair on our housemates to talk too much about our faith. Strangely, the more we prayed, the more we thought, 'Say nothing'. One day, I came in with the shopping and was asked, 'I know you are dying to tell me. What is it about Christianity that means so much to you?'

What a contrast to my previous bad experience of faith-sharing, which had given the impression that we Christians had to do something and other people had to hear it! We were being trained to speak, whether people were interested or not—and if they did not listen, it was not our fault. That moment at university, however, felt like a great joy and privilege, as I was sharing with someone who was interested. It seemed so much more like the 'Jesus way'.

Has your experience of faith-sharing been good or bad? Have you ever been asked difficult questions about faith in a situation where you felt awkward—or a situation that seemed natural? What do you think made the difference?

I love to share my faith, but I never want to force it on anyone. Also, because I am fascinated with evangelism and have seen lives changed, I am always interested in seeing what resources and methods other evangelists employ. I recently met an evangelist (well-intentioned, I am sure) whose approach was to ask one question, which was really designed to launch him into a well-rehearsed script. He spoke for a long time and only took note of anything I said if I was agreeing with him. It was offensive and inconsiderate, and he hadn't even bothered to check first if I was a Christian or not. Once again I thought, 'That's not the way Jesus would do it.'

There are hundreds of definitions of evangelism, but the one I like best is by William Tyndale: '*Evangelion* (that we call the gospel) is a Greek word and signifieth good, merry, glad and joyful tidings, that maketh a man's heart glad, and maketh him sing, dance and leap for joy.'[8] This is a good image to keep in mind when we are thinking of sharing our faith, and it is also a good benchmark by which to check if we and other people are getting it right or not.

Sadly, it is possible to find more examples of how not to speak of Jesus—on the streets, on TV, online, even in some of our churches. Some speakers are compulsive to watch, and they probably bring to faith people whom I shall never reach, but when they entice their audience to receive spiritual blessings by giving money for a 'holy handkerchief' or loaf of bread, I have to say that I think Jesus has left the room. On one occasion, a TV evangelist zapped out the stage lights by pointing at them, to prove that he had the power of the Holy Spirit. I felt that the Spirit of God probably has more important work to do and that the preacher was abusing his privileged position.

I know that the gospel is a challenge and an offence to some people, but, in essence, 'God so loved the world that he gave his one and only Son' (John 3:16). This is a message of love and generosity in forgiveness and eternal life, and need not be manipulated to get a response.

I have said that I'm a member of the Church Army.[9] The Church Army was founded by Wilson Carlile in 1882, with the aim of helping ordinary people to share their faith. Carlile is quoted as saying that many Christians are like Arctic rivers, 'frozen at the mouth'. He would cite 1 Peter 3:15: 'Always be prepared to give an answer to everyone who asks you to give the reason for the hope that you have.' Significantly, however, we should note that the verse continues, 'But do this with gentleness and respect.' Jesus' way is to be natural. As we speak, let's consider what might be helpful for the other person to hear about the good news.

Jesus didn't preach at people or put them down. He engaged with individuals, and would also address a crowd when it gathered. He did not hide the message he had for them, but carefully explained it to those who listened. He did not outstay his welcome, as we can see by the fact that crowds continued to follow him wherever he went. For him, healings and miracles were everyday events, conducted without too much fuss and ceremony. The only fuss came from those who thought he was disobeying God.

Have a look at chapters 1—4 of Mark's Gospel. Consider the different people who encountered Jesus and the way he emphasised different aspects of his message for each individual. In Mark 4:1–20 you will find the parable of the sower and the seed. What does that teach about Jesus and sharing faith? What can we learn from it about success, failure and the skill of the sower? Think, too, about how communication is often more powerful without words. Are there any examples of this principle in Mark 1—4?

To end this section on good and bad experiences of evangelism, here is a story with a twist. Ruth told me that before she was a Christian, she used to get fed up with her neighbour, who was very enthusiastic in talking about faith. In the end, Ruth was pleased to be going away to New Zealand for an extended holiday to see her family. It would give her a break from all her neighbour's 'witnessing'. After the long flight, it was a joy to see her family at the other end, but what happened next was a complete surprise and changed her life for ever. Her little granddaughter came running across the airport concourse with her arms open wide, shouting, 'Nana, do you know Jesus loves you?' Ruth used to join me as a team member and would tell her story, saying, 'I had to go to the other side of the world to find Jesus!'

Follow-up activities

- If you have not done so already, I strongly suggest that you get a notebook to keep track of what you are thinking, reading and doing about sharing faith the Jesus way. You could use it like an ordinary notebook or diary, or be a bit more intentional and leave space for what you feel God might be saying to you. Robin kept a journal and only wrote on the right-hand pages, leaving the left side blank. On the left he would add headings like 'What would Jesus say?' as well as 'To pray for' and 'Answered prayer'.
- If you are reading this book in a church group, consider the various experiences you have had about sharing faith. Make a list of bad and good practices, or try listing your 'Top ten tips to put people off hearing the gospel'.
- If you are a church leader, think about the people in your congregation and how they might be encouraged to share

their faith more effectively. Take a look at the summary series of readings and questions in Appendix C, which could be used as the core of a six-week course for sermons and groups.

Personality matters!

'Come, follow me.'
MARK 1:17

The same breath is blown into the flute, cornet and bagpipe, but different music is produced according to the different instruments. In the same way, the one Spirit works in us, God's children, but different results are produced, and God is glorified through them according to one's temperament and personality.
SADHU SUNDAR SINGH[10]

When Jesus asked people to follow him, he did not go on and check their credentials. While he called them to 'repent and believe', he did not check up to see if they had done it. For the most part, he simply said, 'Follow me.' Some people, as we have seen already, needed a particular message, but there was no 'gold standard' that everyone had to reach before they could be called a disciple. Being a disciple means being a follower.

Nick Baines has written:

The disciples of Jesus followed him with mixed motives and a variety of fantasies. But follow him they did. In one sense, that was all Jesus required of them: start the journey with me, and we'll see what happens along the way. He did not examine their theological soundness or doctrinal purity. He did not criticise their ethics or demand changes in their eschatology before they could come with him. He did not make sure that they would ultimately last the course before inviting them—they would have to choose for themselves whether or not they would go with him to the bitter end. Jesus let them be the people they were, with all their strengths and weaknesses, bringing with them the totality of their personality and character and bearing their own particular life story. They only had to be willing to walk—the rest would follow in due time.[11]

Think of the disciples and consider their varied personalities and outstanding characteristics:

- Simon Peter: impulsive; later bold in preaching about Jesus
- James, son of Zebedee: ambitious, short-tempered, judgmental, deeply committed to Jesus
- John, son of Zebedee: ambitious, judgmental, later very loving
- Andrew, Peter's brother: eager to bring other people to Jesus
- Philip: questioning attitude
- Bartholomew (Nathanael): honest and straightforward
- Matthew (Levi): a despised outcast because of his dishonest career
- Thomas, the twin: courageous and, at the same time, doubting
- James, son of Alphaeus: unknown

- Thaddaeus (Judas son of James): unknown
- Simon the Zealot: fiercely patriotic
- Judas Iscariot: treacherous and greedy

Try to imagine the different personality types of the disciples and how they might have got on together. Do you identify with any one of them in particular?

These disciples may have been a disparate group of people, but they were precisely the ones whom God chose to change the world. Because Jesus brought these men together, today a third of the population on our planet call themselves Christian.[12] What does this say about how God can use different personality types?

Jesus accepted them all. While Peter, James and John were the core group and Judas was a betrayer, nowhere do we read of Jesus saying that any one disciple was better or worse than another. This is hugely important as an illustration of our first principle: 'Jesus accepts you as you are' for his work of passing on the good news. Two thousand years have not changed that principle.

Take a few moments to think about different styles of sharing faith. You may be a great conversationalist or write about the Christian faith in a local magazine. You might represent the church as a school governor or pray for lots of people and encourage them by text and phone. You could have a leaflet or Gospel or Christian book to hand on, or be great at inviting people to events at your church or home group. You could be a full-time carer or run an Alpha course, preach or practise hospitality. You may be passionate about how the gospel relates to a social issue, belong to a reading group or build relationships by pursuing a hobby. The list is endless. People have found faith in Christ through all these channels. Some of these options appeal to different personalities. What is your preference?

Becoming a Contagious Christian is a rare example of a training course that recognises the importance of personality types in sharing our faith. It helpfully lists the following different styles found in the New Testament.

- **Confrontational**: for example, Peter in Acts 2 (along the lines of 2 Timothy 4:2: 'Preach the word; be prepared in season and out of season; correct, rebuke and encourage— with great patience and careful instruction').
- **Intellectual**: for example, Paul in Acts 17 (along the lines of 2 Corinthians 10:5: 'We demolish arguments and every pretension that sets itself up against the knowledge of God, and we take captive every thought to make it obedient to Christ').
- **Testimonial**: for example, the blind man in John 9 (along the lines of 1 John 1:3a: 'We proclaim to you what we have seen and heard, so that you may have fellowship with us').
- **Interpersonal**: for example, Matthew in Luke 5 (along the lines of 1 Corinthians 9:22: 'I have become all things to

all men so that by all possible means I might save some').

- **Invitational**: for example, the woman at the well in John 4 (along the lines of Luke 14:23: 'The master told his servant, "Go out to the roads and country lanes and make them come in, so that my house will be full"').
- **Serving**: for example, Dorcas in Acts 9 (along the lines of Matthew 5:16: 'In the same way, let your light shine before men, that they may see your good deeds and praise your Father in heaven').[13]

Think about these different approaches. What are the relative advantages and disadvantages of each one in terms of sharing faith?

Remembering that Jesus accepts you as you are is a prerequisite to sharing your faith: you have to be yourself. Jesus loves you. Jesus forgives you. Jesus wants to use you—but he also wants to change you. We read that we are 'being transformed into his likeness with ever-increasing glory, which comes from the Lord, who is the Spirit' (2 Corinthians 3:18). We are all different, but we are all to become more like Christ in order to share God's message with the world.

As a bridge to the next chapter, here is an illuminating story about how evangelists and pastors have different personalities but need each other. It shows how evangelists often do unpredictable, edgy things that leave other people with the follow-up!

An evangelist and a pastor go on a trip into the North American wilderness. Having reached their remote cabin in the woods, they settle for a night's sleep. The following morning, the pastor wakes up to discover the evangelist has disappeared. As he gets up to find out where his colleague has gone, the pastor hears frantic shouting from outside the cabin. He looks out of the window and sees the evangelist running for his life down the hill towards the cabin, pursued by a huge grizzly bear. As they approach the cabin, the bear is gaining on the evangelist, who is now screaming for the pastor to open the door, open the door! As the evangelist gets to the door, the pastor throws it open, whereupon the evangelist deftly swerves to the right and the bear, which is right behind him by now, lumbers into the cabin. As the alarmed and now cornered pastor takes rapid stock of the situation, he sees through the open door the evangelist running back up the hill and hears him call over his shoulder, 'You look after that one. I'll go catch some more!' [14]

Follow-up activities

- Read Luke 10:38–42 and think about the encounter between Mary, Martha and Jesus in terms of different personality types. Then read John 11:17–45 and consider what further light it casts on your thinking.
- Imagine a disparate group of people on a camping expedition together. A small group who already know each other are joined by some random individuals, some with strong personalities, needs or opinions. Everyone has a different idea of what to do. Several people are used to being leaders. Some are uncertain about the whole thing and others

begin to be manipulative. Imagine the conversation. Does this exercise cast any light on the twelve disciples of Jesus?

- Finally, as we have been thinking about 'personality types', have you done anything to find out what personality type you are? One of the most well researched and widely used by Christians is the Myers-Briggs Type Indicator (MBTI™), which is a questionnaire-based tool that helps individuals and groups to understand their personality preferences. Each person can be described as one of 16 'types', and no one type is considered to be better than another. Ask around to see if a training day using this tool is available locally.

Chapter 2

Jesus respects the other person and sees their need

'Friend, your sins are forgiven.'
LUKE 5:20

Jesus always met people at their point of need. People will not listen to the gospel message and respond unless it speaks to felt needs. Effective evangelism begins where people are, not where we would like them to be.

JOSEPH ALDRICH [15]

Let's consider another classic text from the Gospels—the story of the paralysed man lowered through the roof to Jesus (Luke 5:17–26). Imagine the man on the mat, and his friends. Who needs friends like that? First they pick him up and carry him to the house, where they find a crowd gathered. Undeterred, they take him up on to the roof. Did the man have a choice? No. Probably paralysed with fear as well as illness by now, he is suddenly thrust into the limelight as the tiles are removed and everyone looks up. I wonder what you would be feeling at this point? Probably a mixture of emotions—embarrassment, fear of falling, and excitement at meeting the healer. And after all this, what does Jesus say? 'Friend, your sins are forgiven'!

In Chapter 1 we considered our first principle: that Jesus accepts us as we are. Now we turn to our second principle: that Jesus has an eye on the particular need of the other person, especially anything that might stop them responding to God's love. If people were hungry, he fed them. If they felt troubled by an evil spirit, he delivered them. If they were ill, he healed them. Different people had different needs and Jesus addressed those needs as necessary. Interestingly, although the man lowered through the roof came looking for physical healing, Jesus met his deeper need—forgiveness of sins. It was only afterwards that he said, 'Get up, take your mat and go home' (v. 24). In the end, the paralysed man got a double blessing.

Read Luke 5:17–26. Imagine yourself in the story, perhaps first as one of the paralysed man's friends trying to get through the crowd to Jesus, and then as the man on the mat being carried and lowered through the roof. Finally, think of yourself as one of the onlookers who had come to see Jesus. Imagine what your reactions might have been in each case, especially when Jesus came out with the startling words about forgiveness and then healing.

Like the friends who put themselves out to help the man on the mat, Jesus also put the needs of the other person first. It is a principle of sharing faith the Jesus way that we do the same, rather than focusing on what we think ought to happen. Jesus knew that the crowd contained critics who would object to both his theology and his practice. Was he concerned about this criticism? No, he would not be distracted by it: the man's needs came first. Jesus was bringing in a new order, and much would change as a result.

In this chapter we shall consider the following:

- Everyday encounters with Jesus
- Jesus' message is not 'one size fits all'
- Exploring the idea of a '360 gospel'

Everyday encounters with Jesus

'I must stay at your house today.'
LUKE 19:5

Intimate friendship with Jesus, on which everything depends.
POPE BENEDICT XVI [16]

As we read the Gospels, we see that Jesus encountered people in their homes, on the road, by the lake, up mountains, and especially at the meal table. In other words, he met people and transformed their lives in all sorts of places and in everyday circumstances, right where they were.

Whom did Jesus meet in the home? Think of the man lowered through the roof (Luke 5:17–26), Mary and Martha (10:38–42), Zacchaeus (19:1–10), or the house where the

Passover was prepared for the last supper (22:7–13). Interestingly, in all of these examples, we note that they involved someone else's house. Jesus did not have a home of his own, of course, so he was used to borrowing other people's.

We also read of Jesus meeting people along the road—for example, Zacchaeus, again, who was up a sycamore-fig tree when Jesus said something both simple and profound to him: 'I must stay at your house today' (Luke 19:5). Their encounter continued in Zacchaeus' home, but it started on the street with an apparently matter-of-fact statement. Among others who met Jesus on the road are the woman who touched his cloak (Mark 5:25–34) and Bartimaeus (10:46–52), as well as the disciples in the resurrection appearance on the road to Emmaus (Luke 24:13–35). Perhaps the most dramatic of all came later, with the conversion of Saul on the Damascus road (Acts 9:1–9).

Jesus met people at their place of work. He was just walking along the shore line when he called his first disciples (Matthew 4:18). The fishermen were minding their own business, without any idea that their lives were about to change. Little did they know that we would be reading their story today, 2000 years later, and that a third of the world's population would be followers of Jesus because of what they did next. It all started with a walk, at a place of work, on a normal working day—an everyday encounter with the most extraordinary outcome.

If we think about it, the way we present the gospel today, in church or at evangelistic events, is more like Jesus visiting the synagogue or preaching the Sermon on the Mount, with a well-thought-out, 'prepared' text being presented to the assembled audience or congregation. Important though these speaking events are, we should think of them as being in addition to the way in which most of the spiritually meaningful encounters happen, in our own day as well as in Jesus' time.

Nicodemus is an interesting case to consider. In John 3, we read that Nicodemus was a Pharisee and a member of the ruling Jewish council, and first came to find Jesus at night. In what Max Lucado calls 'the most famous conversation in the Bible',[17] we see a brief but extraordinary encounter. Nicodemus starts by stating that he knows that Jesus is from God because of the miraculous signs he performs, and straight away Jesus declares, 'I tell you the truth, no one can see the kingdom of God unless he is born again' (v. 3).

You could argue that this conversation was hardly an everyday encounter, because it is surprising that Nicodemus came to Jesus at all. He was taking a huge risk for a man in his position, as Jesus was already posing a threat to the religious authorities. At the same time, the encounter was in an informal setting rather than in a synagogue or the temple precincts. The recorded conversation is very direct and deep, and it instantly engages with theology. The declaration that Nicodemus should be born again was shocking in the extreme—an insult to his religious credentials as a member of the ruling council. Remarkably, though, he does not take offence or call for Jesus to be arrested, but instead engages in the conversation, gradually becoming a believer.

Surely the fruitfulness of this encounter was grounded in the fact that Jesus was prepared to meet Nicodemus on his own terms, including after dark! We do not read of Jesus forcing him to make a decision, forthright though Jesus is in the conversation, and he leaves Nicodemus to work out the implications himself. Nicodemus continues his faith journey without regular meetings with the other disciples (as far as we know), and it is remarkable that he later publicly defends Jesus (John 7:50–52) and is even involved in burying Jesus' body (19:39–40), an act that would have made him ritually unclean for seven days, during the Passover season. All of these things probably made him very unpopular with his own fellow religious leaders.

Nicodemus is a remarkable example of someone who manages compromise and remains faithful at the same time. His is a story that finds an echo today in the lives of many Christians who come from another faith background or live in a country where a public profession of Christian faith is illegal. People can be secret believers in Jesus, despite all the odds, like Nicodemus. God is with them: Jesus is on their side.

Another example of an everyday encounter between Jesus and a faith seeker is to be found in the story of the Roman centurion and his sick servant (Matthew 8:5–13). Surprisingly, the centurion addresses Jesus as 'Lord'—which may have been a treasonable offence—and then asks for his servant to be healed. You might imagine that Jesus would have called the centurion to leave the army, renounce the occupying force and become his follower. Instead, 'astonished' (v. 10) by the centurion's belief in his authority over sickness, Jesus is prepared to heal the servant there and then. Again, we see how he is on the side of the person in need.

God calls people to be evangelists, pioneer ministers, church planters, community workers, church leaders, ministers and preachers. Indeed, you may be one of these kinds of people, or sense the call to be one. This is great, but the point I want to make is that every one called 'Christian' is carrying the name of Christ. Every Christian is a minister of the gospel. We are all in a position to meet people in everyday contexts, and at any time we could be the means by which someone encounters Christ. We are all in ministry and we could be exercising our ministry in a wide variety of everyday situations.

When people meet us, they should see something of Jesus in us. Indeed, we may be the only connection with Jesus that some people ever have. That is a privilege but also a daunting prospect. It is part and parcel of being a follower of Jesus, though, and the place where such connections are made is in everyday encounters with people we know or meet.

Here are two contemporary examples of people who encountered Jesus in the ordinary everyday events of life. In my experience, many people become Christians in this kind of way, and through people like you and me. This is substantiated by the research being conducted by the *Faith Journey* website project and others. While we can thank God for those who come to faith through professional evangelists, ministers, leaders and preachers, we shouldn't let their gifts discourage us from recognising that we too have a key part to play in helping people meet Jesus today.

Ann started work in a new school and was very impressed by some of the staff. Gradually it turned out that they were Christians, and Ann thought to herself, 'I want their faith.' She prayed that she would find a church open for a Sunday evening service, and was pleased to discover that her local church answered that prayer. She began to attend once a month. 'It couldn't come quickly enough,' she says, so she began to attend once a week. 'It changed my life,' she continues. 'Having faith is wonderful, and when my son had a brain haemorrhage I was able to phone round all the people in my cell group to ask them to pray. Thank God, he is recovering and thank God for the Christian friends who prayed.'

Mark's faith journey was very different. Blind since birth, he attended a church-run school where discipline was very strict and he was punished for not learning. As lessons were taught in a different language from his own, which was English, the whole experience was difficult for him and he did not feel sympathetic to the Christian faith. Later, at college, he came across other Christians and joined in their lunch-time discussion groups, which enlivened his faith for two to three years, until eventually he felt 'alienated from Christianity because of relationships and my artistic musical interest, which was seen as "of the devil"'. Much later, Mark, a very talented musician, got involved in various music networks and met Sally, a Christian who invited him to take part in some performances linked to a local church. He had many academic questions about faith and felt able to discuss them with Sally and the people he subsequently met at church. Mark loves to discuss and is very open about his Christian faith. Although he would not think so, he is now a natural evangelist, especially through his musical and other networks.

Just as Ann's and Mark's spiritual needs were met by ordinary Christians in everyday encounters, so you in your turn can help others find Christ. Be encouraged: you may well be a link in the chain.

Think for a moment about your social and professional networks and the people you meet in the course of daily life. Thank God and pray for them.

In their book about evangelism, *Unlocking the Door*, Ruth Adams and Jan Harney write:

Jesus didn't sit in the synagogue waiting for people to come in: he got out and about wherever people were, healing and story telling. We need to follow his example and talk to people about their work, their hobbies, their concerns, and the things that interest them or are relevant to their lives. These will ultimately be the pegs on which we most effectively hang our message. We start where people are and gradually find ways to create a forum for further discussion.[18]

Follow-up activities

- Read the first four chapters of John's Gospel. As you did with Mark's Gospel, see how the principles we have explored are worked out in the life and ministry of Jesus. The two Gospels have very different styles, but can you see the same principles in them, of Jesus accepting people and meeting their needs?
- Take a small piece of card and jot down the names of six people you meet in your everyday life. Keep the card with

you in your wallet or purse so that you are frequently reminded to pray for them.

- Imagine the following situations and ask yourself, 'How would Jesus help these people find faith?' What might you say and do in similar circumstances?

  ❖ You meet up with a group of people you know reasonably well but don't see very often. One of them says, 'Hi, I'm glad to see you. We had two people at the door the other day, talking about religion, and I wondered what you thought about people doing that.'

  ❖ You get to know someone new, and they eventually find out that you are a Christian and go to church. They then say, 'I don't believe in God—well, not the sort of old man in the sky telling us what to do all the time.'

  ❖ You go to visit someone who is seriously ill and they keep asking, 'Why me?'

Jesus' message is not 'one size fits all'

I have become all things to all men so that by all possible means I might save some. I do this for the sake of the gospel, that I may share in its blessings.
1 CORINTHIANS 9:22B–23

Just like the apostle Paul, whose words are quoted above, we have begun to see that Jesus met people where they were, both geographically and at their point of need. He offered a personalised gospel—made clearest, above all, in Jesus himself. God became like one of us to save us, which is what we call the incarnation. It is beautifully described in Philippians 2:5b–8:

Christ Jesus... being in very nature God, did not consider equality with God something to be grasped, but made himself nothing, taking the very nature of a servant, being made in human likeness. And being found in appearance as a man, he humbled himself and became obedient to death—even death on a cross!

In our ministry to others, we are called to serve them so that they might find Jesus. It is their agenda that matters, not ours. It is their need, rather than ours, that we seek to meet. That is the principle laid down by Jesus himself: we address other people as they are, seeing them as individuals and making the message relevant to them.

Yes, Jesus addressed huge crowds, wept for the whole city of Jerusalem and was a herald of the coming kingdom of God, but in the middle of all this corporate and cosmic concern he could still meet the need of the individual coming to him in faith. Even when pressed in by a throng of people, Jesus responded to an individual woman who touched his cloak (Luke 8:42–48).

'Who touched me?' (v. 45). It is a profound question, addressed initially to the crowd and then to the woman herself. It may sound like a simple enquiry, but it is packed full of meaning and expectation. It is another example of the good news being made personal. Instead of blanket doctrinal statements, we see a tailor-made conversation with the disciples and a woman in need. Interestingly, this episode comes in the middle of another conversation and another enormous need—that of Jairus and his twelve-year-old daughter who was dying.

In both instances, Jesus focuses on the human need for healing. Even when competing demands come at the same time, he is able to manage both. Although he may have kept Jairus waiting for a while, in the end both needs were met and both encounters bore gospel fruit.

While there is nothing radical in recognising how Jesus met different needs and responded to people in different ways, what is surprising (and a challenge to some evangelists) is that he adapted the message to suit the need. The core message was essentially the same, but the aspect presented spoke straight to the particular individual. This contrasts to some extent, I would suggest, with the preaching of Peter and, especially, Paul. In different ways, they both formulated the gospel message within a framework of systematic theology after the death and resurrection of Christ. Paul's preaching, in particular, has often been taken as the norm for evangelism. Let's consider their approaches for a moment.

Peter preached on the day of Pentecost, 'God has made this Jesus, whom you crucified, both Lord and Christ'. The crowd asked in response, 'What shall we do?' and Peter replied, 'Repent and be baptised, every one of you, in the name of Jesus Christ for the forgiveness of your sins. And you will receive the gift of the Holy Spirit' (Acts 2:36–38).

Paul's message was similar, again shaped by the death and resurrection of Jesus, and also, no doubt, profoundly influenced by his own dramatic conversion experience on the Damascus road. An example of Paul's gospel message is found in Romans 3:22–26:

This righteousness from God comes through faith in Jesus Christ to all who believe. There is no difference, for all have sinned and fall short of the glory of God, and are justified freely by his grace through the redemption that came by Christ Jesus. God presented him as a sacrifice of atonement, through faith in his blood. He did this to demonstrate his justice… so as to be just and the one who justifies those who have faith in Jesus.

Unlike Paul, Jesus did not expand the theology of words like election, justification, redemption and sanctification. Rather, he conversed with the woman at the well or taught the parable of the good Samaritan.

I don't mean to set up Paul in opposition to Jesus, as all of this is part of an even bigger picture, but I do want to recognise the difference in emphasis and suggest that we should look primarily to Jesus for our example, especially as I believe that the Jesus way connects with more people today. The message of Jesus addresses all the same needs, but Jesus' way of communicating it was with story, parable, metaphor and illustration, often in a two-way conversation. Faith is often 'caught' rather than 'taught'.

This is a great quote used by the evangelist J John (printed below with permission) to illustrate how Jesus was 'all things to all people'. It is a great picture of the '360' gospel of Jesus.

He's the Bread of Life so that bakers can understand.
    He's the Water of Life so that plumbers can understand.
    He's the Light of the World so that electricians can understand.
    He's the Cornerstone so that architects can understand.
    He's the Sun of Righteousness so that astronomers can understand.

He's the Hidden Treasure so that bankers can understand.
He's the Life so that biologists can understand.
He's the Door so that carpenters can understand.
He's the Great Physician so that doctors and nurses can understand.
He's the Teacher so that educationalists can understand.
He's the Lily of the Valley so that florists can understand.
He's the Rock of Ages so that geologists can understand.
He's the True Vine so that horticulturalists can understand.
He's the Righteous One so that judges can understand.
He's the Pearl of Great Price so that jewellers can understand.
He is Wisdom so that philosophers can understand.
He is the Word so that actors can understand.
He is the Shepherd so that farmers can understand.
He is the Alpha and Omega so that scientists can understand.
He is the Way so that traffic wardens can understand.
He is the Truth so that politicians can understand!

It may sound revolutionary to say that there is no 'one size fits all' message from Jesus, but different aspects of the same message will connect with people where they are. If you think about it, though, we do the same thing naturally. Even on the phone, we often accommodate the other person—to the extent that, if they have a strong accent, we sometimes find ourselves beginning to sound the same as they do! It is well known that if we are listening to someone carefully, we tend to mirror their movements, subliminally indicating that we are warming to them.

If you ask three evangelists today for an explanation of the gospel, I suspect that you will get three different answers—

perhaps because of the way in which they understand and interpret the gospel, but also because they are considering who they are speaking to. This is illustrated by Bishop Tom Wright on a blog site dedicated to definitions of the gospel. Tom Wright himself is quoted as having given four definitions in different books, lectures and magazine articles. A student of his asks for a summary of the gospel—and is given a fifth.[19]

I suspect that all of us colour our presentation of the Christian faith according to our own personal experience of coming to Christ. At one time I was a tutor, teaching evangelism studies at the Church Army College, and it was very interesting to observe the students in this regard. I could see how people who had been convinced of the gospel by a preacher often wanted to preach themselves. Those who had come to faith through counselling often wanted to show similar care to others.

Bill Hybels illustrates this point well. Describing how he came to Christ, he says he remembers exactly where he was standing when he took 'that critical step'. He tells how he had a clear picture of the heavenly rejoicing in Luke 15:10: 'There was an enormous party with the honouree's name on the banner—and it was mine! When that dawned on me, I remember thinking, "I must really matter to God"!'[20] Perhaps not surprisingly, Hybels' first chapter in his book *Becoming a Contagious Christian* is entitled 'People matter to God'. Later, he says that when he explains the gospel, 'I usually start by saying, "We matter to God."'[21]

Jesus gave various instructions on how to be a follower, and he also gave two different answers to the same question.

As I mentioned in the Introduction, two people on separate occasions asked, 'What must I do to inherit eternal life?' To one, a teacher of the law, Jesus told the parable of the good Samaritan and suggested that the teacher should be the one who cared for others (Luke 10:25–37). To the other man, a rich young ruler, he gave an economic answer, saying that he should give away his goods to the poor, and illustrated his answer with the picture of a camel and the eye of a needle (Luke 18:18–30).

Can you see that the gospel according to Jesus is not 'one size fits all'? Is this a comfort or a challenge to your understanding of the gospel?

Follow-up activities

- Begin to collate some faith journey stories from people you know, especially if they go to another church or have a very different experience or understanding of the Christian faith from yours. Thank God that each story is different, and see if any similarities exist between them.
- Visit the *Faith Journeys* website again and look at the 'tag cloud' that accompanies each story. The tag cloud is an interesting illustration of the key words in the story and their significance. The more often the word occurs, the bigger the word in the 'cloud', so that, at a glance, you get an illustration of the elements of the story. You will see that every one is different. (Note: if you contribute your story

to the *Faith Journeys* website, you don't have to allow it to be made public on the site.)

The 360 gospel of Jesus

'I am the Alpha and the Omega, the First and the Last, the Beginning and the End.'
REVELATION 22:13

'I am the way and the truth and the life.'
JOHN 14:6

In their book *Conversions*, Hugh T. Kerr and John M. Mulder have considered faith journeys through church history to the present day. They observe that 'there is a remarkable, even exhilarating, variety in the way people describe their conversions' and go on to illustrate with some examples.

Sometimes the experience is primarily moral, leading the person from a life that is seen as sinful or wrong into a pattern of behaviour and a vision of existence that emphasises obedience, discipline, social justice. But at other times the experience seems to be aesthetic rather than moral—a glimpse of the beauty of holiness and a new way of perceiving the world and one's place in it. Some emphasise the power of God and their surrender to God's amazing grace, while others stress the decision they made to accept the forgiveness that was offered to them in Jesus Christ.[22]

Professor James Denney of Scotland once said that Jesus probably repeated himself 500 times—to which Billy Graham added the comment, 'Don't assume a truth has stuck with your listeners just because you have mentioned it once; hammer home the basic points of the gospel repeatedly.'[23] Much as I admire and respect the amazing influence of Dr Graham, I shall dare to disagree with him on this point. My reading of the four Gospels does not highlight repetition of the basic points but an application of a particular aspect of the good news, addressing individual need.

As we have seen, Jesus met all manner of needs. If someone was hungry, he gave them food. If they were sick, he offered healing. If they were possessed, he brought deliverance. However, we have already seen in the story of the man lowered through the roof that Jesus addressed the need for forgiveness before telling the man to take up his mat and go home. In a reverse scenario, when the teacher of the law came with a spiritual question about eternal life, he was told to go and be a good neighbour.

We touched on the issue of the 'deeper need' at the start of this chapter, but it would be good to consider it further here. What is the deeper need? I suggested that it was whatever gets in the way of people's response to God's love. Hunger is an obvious example. Of course, people will not listen to words if their stomachs are empty. In the same way, we can fail to receive all that God wants to give us if we are full of sin. Both the hunger and the sin get in the way, and they are both needs that Jesus wants to address. The question is, which needs should be addressed first? Sometimes it will be the more obvious or urgent, and sometimes the deeper or more fundamental.

If you wrote them down, take a few minutes to look at the headlines of your faith story—or your timeline, if you drew one. What needs were being met at what times? Are there still needs to be addressed? Take time to pray and ask Jesus to address these needs. Slowly read Isaiah 43:1: 'Fear not, for I have redeemed you: I have summoned you by name; you are mine.'

If Jesus presented different aspects of his core message to different people, depending on their need, we should take some time to consider that core, essential message.

Robin Gamble has cogently argued in *Jesus the Evangelist* that Jesus was not only an evangelist but (not surprisingly) the best of evangelists: 'Evangelistic opportunity and ministry derive from Jesus. He did it first, and remains the best model for us to learn from.'[24] With regard to the message of the gospel that Jesus preached, Robin says:

Frustratingly, we do not possess any straight proclamation-type sermons or stories to study and copy. What we do have is not so much detailed content as banner headlines:

Good news!
The kingdom of God is here!'
Repent and believe!

He goes on to say:

These three topics do not arrange themselves into a neat formula or sequence; instead they should be seen much more as a sort of fluid zone in which Jesus the Proclaimer moves around. Our task, then, is to flesh out these big brassy trumpet blasts and see how they can become the basis for our evangelistic message today.[25]

Building on the core message that Robin helpfully identifies for us, I want to 'flesh out these big brassy trumpet blasts'. To continue his musical metaphor, I want to get the full orchestral score!

Looking at the Gospels as they have been handed down to us, and taking care not to re-count the passages that are repeated in more than one Gospel, I considered all the words of Jesus that might have been an answer to the question 'What must I do to inherit eternal life?' and drew up a list of 84 texts. To leave out the more debatable answers to the question and to make the list more manageable, I decided to cut it down to the 'Top Fifty', which illustrate the big picture, or full orchestral score, of the overall message that Jesus presented.

If you have not done so already, have a look at Appendix A, where you can find this list.

Don't worry; you don't have to remember 50 Bible texts! You don't even have to get too stressed about discerning the precise need of the other person. God does that, and all we have to do is to pray and rely on the Holy Spirit. I know it may sound too simplistic, but it really is as straightforward as that. When it comes to the 'big picture', I want to suggest a little image to help you think of the great gift that Jesus has for each one of us. It is the image of a diamond with its many facets, each gleaming bright as it reflects and refracts the light shining through it from different angles. Like a diamond, the gospel can be viewed from many different angles. Each facet is part of the whole.

Of course, the image of a diamond is one of beauty: it is also one of value. Because a diamond is precious, it reminds me of the parable of the pearl of great price: 'The kingdom of heaven is like a merchant looking for fine pearls. When he found one of great value, he went away and sold everything he had and bought it' (Matthew 13:45).

'The whole church taking the whole gospel to the whole world' is the phrase used by the international Lausanne Movement for World Evangelisation.[26] It is a helpful phrase to remember, as it describes the 360 picture perfectly. You and I are part of the 'whole church' and it is Jesus' call on us to think about the 'whole gospel' and to share it wherever we meet people in the 'whole world'. The Lausanne Movement is part of the World Evangelical Alliance, so it is good to see a similar quote from Bishop Michael Marshall, who speaks from the Catholic tradition: 'So we might take our working definition of Catholic evangelism as something like: "nothing less than the whole gospel for the whole person and the whole created order".'[27]

I wonder if you are asking yourself, 'That's fine, but what exactly is the gospel?' It's brilliant to think about how the gospel relates to everyone in one way or another, but can we define it? What, if you like, is at the heart of the diamond? Let me offer you my own summary, which I share whenever anyone asks me that question.

Essentially, the Christian faith is about God's love for the world, which is focused in the person of Jesus. His death on the cross provides forgiveness of our sins, and his resurrection makes new life possible for us. The Holy Spirit brings us that new life and the church is the place where we learn, help and encourage one another. A phrase I use in conversation is 'God's love, forgiveness and new life', which, for me, is a shorthand explanation of what the gospel is, both from the perspective of Jesus and Paul, who tell us a lot more about these great themes in their preaching and letters to the new churches.

We could all come up with a slightly different summary or present a different facet of the gospel, but, for me, 'God's love, forgiveness and new life' is something I can use in conversation. It is also a framework for explaining the gospel on the basis of the Trinity:

- **God the Father:** who loved and loves us
- **God the Son:** Jesus, who died on the cross so that we can receive forgiveness
- **God the Holy Spirit:** who empowers and sustains our new life in Christ.

In the next chapter, we shall look at God's love as the key principle behind sharing faith the Jesus way. Remember the triangle of relationships in the Introduction? In Chapter 1 we thought about you, and in this chapter we have focused more on the other person in that triangle. Now we will turn our attention to the top of the triangle and God's love for us in Jesus, which is central to the good news of the gospel.

Follow-up activities

- Reflect on your journey of faith and ask yourself, 'Which facet of the Christian gospel has been most relevant to me?'
- Have a look in Appendix A at the Top Fifty texts that Jesus gave to different people. Make a note of the three that speak most clearly to you and your own faith journey— one for the past, one for now and one that gives you hope for the future. If you are chatting with a friend about this book, you could both do the exercise and then compare notes.
- If you are a church leader, consider using the above exercise with a group or congregation. It is interesting to do and can provide some helpful insights. The Top Fifty texts are also available in a questionnaire on the website that accompanies this book (www.jesus360.org.uk).

Chapter 3

God's love is the key to the gospel

*For God so loved the world that he gave his one and only
Son, that whoever believes in him shall not perish but have
eternal life.*
JOHN 3:16

*And now these three remain: faith, hope and love. But the
greatest of these is love.*
1 CORINTHIANS 13:13

In sharing faith the Jesus way, our task is to let people know
that God's story is a love story. God is love. Jesus came
because of God's love. We go where God sends us because
of God's love. It is as simple as that. God's love is the key
message, and all we have to do is help people respond to it.

As Christians, we have responded to God's love in Christ;
our prayer is that others will respond and know love, forgiveness and new life in Christ, too. Once, when I took the
funeral of an old lady called Ethel, I was delighted to see that
she had written in her Bible, 'God so loved the world that he
gave his one and only Son, that Ethel, who believes in him,
shall not perish but have eternal life.'

Read John 3:16 aloud to yourself and place your own name in the verse.

We have seen, in several Gospel readings, that Jesus overturned people's expectations of him. He was full of surprises. He challenged their views and gave them unexpected new insights. He cared when others walked away, and he remembered those who were ignored or forgotten. He turned the cultural, religious and legal practices of his day upside down. Why? It was all down to God's love.

As Christians, we are called to follow in the footsteps of Jesus. We are to do his work with him as our guide, the 'author and perfecter of our faith' (Hebrews 12:2)—and we do not have to do this in our own strength but with the Holy Spirit, who is always with us. The great commission to 'go and make disciples' is immediately followed by the promise, 'Surely I am with you always' (Matthew 28:19–20). God's love is with us and with all our relations and friends and acquaintances, as they are loved by him, too.

When we are sharing our faith, both our words and our actions should be characterised by love. Love is the first element of the good news; it is the key to people listening, receiving and understanding the truth of the gospel.

An important reading for this chapter is the parable of the lost son (Luke 15:11–32). With this message in mind, in this chapter we shall think of:

- The triangle of relationships with God's love as the key
- A simple model of two-way communication
- How to respond to God's love in Jesus

The triangle of relationships with God's love as the key

Let's go back to the point made in the introduction to this book—that essentially there are three stories involved in the faith-sharing process. There is your story, the other person's story and God's story. At the top of the triangle is God's love in Jesus for you and the other person.

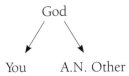

Recently, I have been listening to a number of Christians tell their stories. I was struck by the fact that, at one point, four of them in succession said that 'being bullied' was a significant part of their faith journey. For them, finding God's love in God's people was part of their healing.

This is Emma's story in her own words:

The bullies would tell me that I was nothing and that I would not do anything in my life, that I was useless, thick, and stupid. I believed them. When I left school, I felt I had nothing in my life. Every day was a struggle. When I was about 17, I turned to drink. I would go out every night and at the end of the evening I would be drunk. This carried on for many years. Then I felt I could not carry on, so I tried to kill myself. I tried twice and was angry when I failed at that as well. I ended up in a psychiatric hospital and it took a long time till I felt better, but I still felt that I was useless and a failure.

Then, over four years ago, I was made redundant from work. I did not know what to do. I had a mortgage and how could I cope? That week, I kept thinking 'go to church' and I kept saying, 'Why would I want to go to church? That's not for me', but the feelings got stronger. Then one Sunday I did go to church. After the service, somebody prayed for me. As I was so upset, I just broke down. She prayed that I'd get a job, and two weeks later I did get a job and I am still there now.

I have been to church ever since. I have got confidence to do things. I have been an Alpha leader and done a course on prayer ministry. I have achieved so much and I know that I am not useless. I have felt God at work in my life so much, helping me and restoring me, and I love him so much.

A Bible passage that helps us think about all this is Luke 15:11–32, where Jesus tells the parable of the lost son, sometimes known as the prodigal son. It is also sometimes renamed the parable of the loving father, as that gives us a better sense of the emphasis in the story. While some of us identify most with the prodigal son, and others may sense an affinity with the elder brother, we are all called to emulate the love of the father.

Read Luke 15, where you will find three parables: the lost sheep, the lost coin and the lost son. What similarities strike you about them—and what differences?

Let's look in detail at the parable of the lost son / loving father. Here we note some headlines from the parable, which illustrate God's love in Jesus for us.

- In Jesus' day it was unthinkable for a son to ask for his inheritance while his father was still alive. It was like saying that he wished his father was dead. In the story, however, the father accepts this implicit suggestion and is generous enough to grant the request, even though it would have made him look foolish to his friends.
- The younger son's unacceptable behaviour in the 'distant country' (v. 13) was to be anticipated when he asked for his inheritance and said he was going away. This does not deter the father from complying.
- The father spends a long time hoping for his son's return. When he finally sees the son coming home, he gathers up his robe and runs. This would suggest that his legs might have been exposed for others to see—an action very unbecoming for a man of his age and an embarrassment in the eyes of the local community. His love was greater than any such embarrassment.
- The father would have been expected to deliver a public rebuke to his son, at the very least. Instead, there is no criticism of the son, not even a 'told you so' comment.

Rather, there is a public embrace that says it all. Despite what others might have said or done, the father is overwhelmed with love and gratitude that his son has returned, and is not afraid to show it.

- The father's love next shows itself in the extravagant feast he orders, in which there are no half measures and even the fattened calf is brought out. This is astonishing, especially as, at this point, it is apparent that the older brother doesn't know what is going on. The father's joy compels him to prepare the feast before thinking of the possible consequences.

- The older son comes in after the feast has started. In his anger, he embodies the exact opposite of the father's love. There is a further surprise, however, when the father pleads for the older son to offer the same generous welcome to the runaway. Bear in mind that this exchange probably takes place in front of all the guests.

- The older son's behaviour is ugly but perfectly understandable. I have heard it described as 'truth spoken out of place'. Although he had good grounds for resentment, however, he was being self-righteous. The father's love continues to shine out as he accepts and understands his older son's response.

This story raises all kinds of questions. Here are some for your own reflection, or for discussion if you are using this book in a group.

- How do we continue to love someone when they have really hurt us?

- How do we welcome the hungry, destitute and repentant 'prodigal'?
- What if the person is not repentant but comes asking for more?
- Presumably forgiveness wasn't hard for the father because he loved his son, but what about the people we don't like?
- Are we ever like the elder son?
- Presumably the father embarrassed himself by running to his son. In our own situations, to what extent are we willing to 'run'?

There's one final point before we move on: God's love is not dependent on our response. He still loves us even if we ignore him, hate him or get things wrong. Remember Peter in the courtyard, denying Jesus (Matthew 26:69–75)? We are Christians only because we have been forgiven. Remember the parable of the sower and the different responses to the sowing of the seed (Mark 4:1–9)? Three-quarters of the seed was 'wasted', whether eaten by the birds, choked by the thorns or scorched by the sun. The parable suggests, though, that this seed was still worth sowing.

Follow-up activities

- Read 1 Corinthians 13, about 'the most excellent way' of love. If you can, read it slowly out loud. Imagine you are going to preach on the passage, and list the main headings that you might use. Ask yourself, 'What is this all about and how does it work in practice?'

- Can you identify somebody you particularly struggle to like? Pray for them and for your relationship—for God's love, forgiveness and new life. Repeat the prayer each day for a week.
- Who are the unlovable or the left out in your community or your church? Try to work out why exactly they don't fit in, and pray for them. Reflect on whether there is anything that you (or other people you know) could do to improve the situation.

A simple model of two-way communication

One of them, an expert in the law, tested him with this question: 'Teacher, which is the greatest commandment in the Law?' Jesus replied, "'Love the Lord your God with all your heart and with all your soul and with all your mind." This is the first and greatest commandment. And the second is like it: "Love your neighbour as yourself." All the Law and the Prophets hang on these two commandments.'
MATTHEW 22:35–40

'Love your neighbour as yourself' is a maxim for many people, a benchmark by which they live, even if they do not know that it comes from the Bible. As we seek to share faith the Jesus way, we need to recognise that people are often good and well-meaning. They are not like the wasteful, runaway son in Jesus' parable. We are all sinners in need of repentance, and so our approach should be chiefly one of acceptance, even if we disagree with what others do or say. The Jesus way is to say, 'I am on your side.'

Craig tells a story about his friend Frank. They were both students in training to be Church Army evangelists and went to a pub for a meeting. Frank got the drinks and kept Craig waiting for quite a long time. When Frank finally came back, Craig asked him, 'How did you do that? I saw you chatting for ages with that big biker fellow by the bar. How did you start the conversation?' Frank said, 'I just assumed that he was a Christian!'

Take a moment to think of the people you know. What is your assumption about their relationship with God? If you know what their relationship is, pray for them. If you don't, pray as well.

How do we share faith the Jesus way? We have thought about how Jesus had an eye for the need of the other person and presented the facet of the gospel most relevant to that need. We have also seen that God's love is the heart of the gospel. The next part of the process is to see what happens when we share our faith. Put simply, it is the coming together of their story with our story as part of God's story.

It is reassuring to know that, essentially, it is God who is the evangelist. Our task is to assist him. Further, it is not that the church has a mission and we ask Jesus to join in it. The mission is God's mission in his world and, as members of his church, we are invited to get involved in it.

We love only because God loved us first. He is the source of love, and our faith-sharing should be an overflow of that love to other people—not necessarily because we are personally fond of them, but because God loves them. Part of our love for them is to name the source of that love.

This simple model of communication theory helps me to think about what is happening when we have a conversation or dialogue. People have applied it to all sorts of situations in education, industry and technology, but few have done so in relation to evangelism. I think it is foundational, however, and illustrates the Jesus way very well.

The diagram below should be very much more complex than this, but it gives the gist of the model. The diagram illustrates two people having a two-way conversation with words in a particular environment. As the dialogue continues, other things can get in the way and act as a barrier, or filter, to what they are saying to each other.

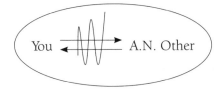

For example, if you are chatting with someone on a train, the conversation takes place in the environment formed by the carriage and the people around you. Now imagine you and the other person are on either side of a table with a laptop playing a DVD between you. The DVD will act as a filter, as you cannot speak and hear each other properly.

Think about how the two-way model of communication works for you. Think of different conversations you have had recently and identify the environment and any filters to effective speaking and listening. Think about whether the balance was right for each situation and whether your relationship with the other person was strengthened or weakened. Do you think you heard the other person and said what you wanted to say?

In John 4, we saw Jesus having a two-way conversation with the woman at the well. The environment was a public place in the open air, in the heat of the day. One of the many filters in this exchange was a cultural one—the strangeness of a Jewish man speaking to a Samaritan woman. The two-way communication took place at different levels, both verbal (Jesus asking for water) and non-verbal (spending time with an outcast when the disciples had gone off to find food).

It goes without saying that a two-way conversation is a key to building good relationships, and it is through a relationship that people hear and experience the good news of the gospel. The relationship does not have to be very deep or last a long time, but it does have to be there. You would not expect to walk down the street, ignore someone you know and still hope to build a good relationship with them.

Take another look at the parable of the good Samaritan in Luke 10:25–37. Arguably, it is one of the most familiar parables in scripture, but it is easy to miss the context and the whole point of the story. We think of it as a description of how to be a good neighbour, while forgetting the original question put to Jesus by the expert in the law: 'Teacher,' he said, 'what must I do to inherit eternal life?' (v. 25). The context is a conversation, and the whole point is that Jesus is addressing the specific need of the individual who asked, 'What must I do?' To another person, Jesus may well have provided an entirely different answer. Sharing faith the Jesus way is about having a conversation with people and addressing their particular needs.

If we look at the number of times Jesus used dialogue and asked questions in his evangelism, we will probably be surprised. One study suggests that the number of times Jesus is quoted in question-and-answer form in each Gospel is:

Matthew 94
Mark............. 59
Luke 82
John .... 49 [28]

Allowing for the duplicate accounts in Matthew, Mark and Luke, there are 159 different questions on the lips of Jesus. The whole point of the Jesus way is to pray, think of God's love for other people, and be ready for a conversation, remaining sensitive to the need of the one to whom we are speaking, and open to the way that need can be met in Jesus.

In short, evangelise as you would like to be evangelised! Conversation provides this check and balance. If you preach at people, you don't know what they are thinking. At this point, you may be asking, 'What if people are not interested?' The simple answer is: don't preach at them, establish common ground, consider things of joint interest, build a good relationship, and demonstrate God's love. This building of relationship, of course, should be for its own sake, never manipulative. Friends soon detect if love is not genuine. But be ready, because the time may come when someone could ask a question, even if it is as simple as 'Well, do you go to church, then?' The more we pray, the more likely we are to have a natural conversation.

I love these words from *The Biblical Foundations for Mission*:

Today no one should be doomed to think of 'mission' in propagandist terms. Missionary activity involves much more than 'making converts', as most missionaries can testify. By 'mission' in this book we mean the God-given call to appreciate and share one's religious experience and insights, first within one's own community and tradition, and then with people and communities of other cultural, social and religious traditions. In so doing, Christians attempt to fulfil the divine mandate given to the church that humanity reflect God's own life as one people drawn together in love and respect. Such a notion means that mission is two-way: faith is shared not imposed, and the missionary will be instructed and enriched by discovering God's salvation already at work in the people and culture to whom he or she is sent. This dialectical pattern rules out any imperious forcing of a religious system on individuals or communities. The gospel comes in the person and message of the missionary as a free and respectful invitation.[29]

(Note: today we would use the term 'mission-partner' rather than 'missionary', precisely because some missionary work has not illustrated the two-way principle.)

In the next section, we shall see just how God's love in Jesus can be a 'free and respectful invitation'.

Follow-up activities

- Go back to the headlines of your own faith journey story. Imagine how you would tell a friend what had happened so far, first in one minute, then in two minutes, and finally in three minutes. I have often heard it said that if you cannot get a point across in three minutes, you will never get it across.
- Have a personal 'theme for the week'. Church leaders who speak several times a week to different audiences often do this. They work on one idea for a talk in one place and then adjust it for another; I have done it myself. You might not be a public speaker but you could develop a habit of thinking in the same way. It could give you the opportunity to say in a conversation, 'That fits with what I have been thinking this week, which is...'
- If you are studying this book in a group, split into threes. Each person takes it in turn to be a speaker, listener or observer for a set of five-minute exercises. In the first of these, the speaker talks to the listener for three minutes on the subject 'Hobbies are great because...' or 'Christianity is important because...' When the three minutes are up, the observer says in just a couple of minutes what they noticed about the communication process: whether there were any questions and answers, illustrations, engagement, and so on. Swap roles for the next five minutes and then move round until everyone has taken a turn in every role.[30]

God's love evokes a response

There is no fear in love.
1 JOHN 4:18A

Love so amazing, so divine, demands my soul, my life, my all.
ISAAC WATTS

We have established that God's love is at the top of the triangle of relationships and he loves us all. We have responded to his love and become disciples as illustrated by the double arrows on the left side. We, in our turn, love other people and pray for a two-way conversation that builds a good relationship in which we can listen to their story and share our story with them.

God

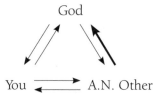

You   A.N. Other

The whole point of sharing faith the Jesus way is to help people make their own response to God's love in Jesus. This is illustrated by the arrow on the far right of the diagram above. It is what God wants; it is what Jesus died for. It should be the focus of our prayer and intention. We are not to force our friends and acquaintances to become Christians—far from it—but we are to be available as we pray for them. We can then help them respond to Jesus in their own way as he invites them.

Before we go on, we need to recap some issues we have already explored in relation to people's response to Christ. The most obvious point to make is that their responses will be different—even quite different from ours. We are not sharing our faith to make people more like us, but more like Jesus. Remember that we are links in a chain: you may even be a crucial link, but there will be others who influence a person's journey to faith. We should also remember that the journey will not be a straight line but will be full of ups and downs.

One of the first people who responded to God's love in Jesus was Peter. Jesus' first words to Peter were, 'Come, follow me' (Mark 1:17) and his last words were, 'You must follow me' (John 21:22). Between these two points, Peter lived a surprising adventure of faith with many ups and downs. He was 'up' when he witnessed the great catch of fish after he had been fishing all night and caught nothing (Luke 5:1–11), 'up' when he witnessed the healing of his mother-in-law (Mark 1:29–31), 'up' when Jesus told him he would be a rock (Matthew 16:18), and 'down' when he nearly drowned (14:30) or was almost arrested (26:69–75). Even in his failures, Jesus accepted Peter, restored him and finally, by the power of the Holy Spirit, empowered him to preach the sermon on the day of Pentecost that precipitated astonishing growth for the new Jesus movement (Acts 2:14–41).

With Jesus, there is always something else to discover or do; another step on the journey and a new 'up' after another 'down'. One reason why Christians can get stagnant in their faith, and then find it difficult to share, is that their own personal journey has slowed down. In Chapter 6 we shall see how that journey can be revitalised. For the moment, though, let's look at the stories of some people who have responded to God's love in Jesus, demonstrated by ordinary Christians today.

Bob Taylor told his story in the magazine *Inspire*,[31] about how his life was transformed at the Kings Arms project in Bedford, after nine years of homelessness. He said:

It was the toaster that did it for me. All I needed was a toaster and when one turned up which matched the kettle and the tea, coffee and sugar pots, I couldn't call it coincidence any more. The staff were really good. They were Christians and told me God loved me. I wasn't sure so I said, 'God, if you really exist, give me a flat.' Within a month I had a flat! When the toaster arrived I gave in and committed my life to God.

On the *Faith Journeys* website, Rob tells his story of God's love for him, sparked by a thought from a surprising source.

During my first week at my first job in Leicester, I walked into the Guildhall and saw inscribed in gold-leaf paint on the wall a verse from Ecclesiastes (12:13), 'Fear God and keep his commandments, for this is the whole duty of man.' That His word seemed to utter forth from a building left me dumbfounded. He is utterly without compare. He still surprises, showers, refreshes and surrounds me with His love. No matter what, He has restored peace to my soul. Looking back… I was a misguided agnostic searching, down any avenue imaginable, for intimacy with a Father who dared to call me His own. In my foolishness and after much pain and confusion, I have discovered that He is my strength, my portion, my wisdom.

Jesus generally looked for a response from people, but, if they were not prepared to give it, he did not go chasing after them. Remember Nicodemus? Like him, we are not forced but invited to respond. We are not made to feel guilty but called to respond to God's love with our love. Of course, there were many people who opposed or ignored Jesus; there were even those who received his healing and just disappeared, like nine out of the ten lepers who were healed on one occasion (Luke 17:11–19). Significantly, in this story, the only one who responded with gratitude was a Samaritan, to whom Jesus said, 'Rise and go; your faith has made you well' (v. 19).

The title of this section is 'God's love evokes a response'. The word 'evokes' is carefully chosen because, while a response is not forced, neither is God's love passive. Jesus did not approach the fishermen and say 'By the way, I don't know if you are interested or not, but I plan to do some work and it would be great if you wanted to leave your nets, your livelihood and your father, and come along to see what I am going to do. No money, of course, but it could be fun to see what happens.' We read that he just said 'Come, follow me' (Matthew 4:19). The invitation was presented with gentle authority, and the fishermen were expected to respond.

Today it is easy to assume that we simply have to be nice to people and hope they come to church. We hesitate about saying things for fear of causing offence or embarrassment— but this is not the Jesus way. Yes, he was warm and inviting, accepting people for who they were, but he was also looking for a response. When he addressed the specific need of another person, it was so that they could respond to God's love.

Follow-up activities

- Search on the internet for an image of Rembrandt's painting *Return of the Prodigal Son* and look at the different characters. What is Rembrandt bringing out from the Gospel story about the father, son and older brother? Think about the person in the shadows, behind the pillar and on the right. Notice the difference between the father's two hands—one hard and one soft, illustrating the two sides of love. For a meditation about this painting and the Gospel story, take a look at Henri Nouwen's book *The Return of the Prodigal Son*.

- Slowly read this famous poem:

Love bade me welcome; yet my soul drew back,
Guilty of dust and sin.
But quick-eyed Love, observing me grow slack
From my first entrance in,
Drew nearer to me, sweetly questioning
If I lacked anything.

'A guest,' I answered, 'worthy to be here.'
Love said, 'You shall be he.'
'I, the unkind, ungrateful? Ah, my dear,
I cannot look on thee.'
Love took my hand, and smiling did reply,
'Who made the eyes but I?'

'Truth, Lord, but I have marred them; let my shame
  Go where it doth deserve.'
'And know you not,' says Love, 'who bore the blame?'
  'My dear, then I will serve.'
'You must sit down,' says Love, 'and taste my meat.'
  So I did sit and eat.

LOVE (III), GEORGE HERBERT (1633) [32]

- Rewrite the poem in your own words, bearing in mind
  that George Herbert was often reflecting on his personal
  experience. His father died when he was three; he did not
  enjoy good health, and he was conscious of his own sin in
  the light of the love of God. This was a personal reflection
  for Herbert: many of his poems were not discovered until
  after he died. Make your rewrite a personal reflection too,
  either using the framework of 'Love bade me welcome', or
  in entirely your own words.
- Discuss both the Rembrandt painting and the George
  Herbert poem in your group or with a friend.
- Finally, choose your favourite song or hymn. If you have
  started a journal, make a note of why this particular choice
  is important to you.

Chapter 4

Prayer, care, and share good news

'My prayer is not for them alone. I pray also for those who will believe in me through their message.'
JOHN 17:20

I have often been asked the secret of evangelistic crusades, and I have said there are three secrets:
- *Prayer*
- *Prayer*
- *Prayer*

BILLY GRAHAM [33]

How are people likely to respond to God's love for them? I want to suggest three essential ingredients: 'prayer, care and share'.

My church minister, Robin, suggested we add 'dare' to the end of this list. Do we dare to share our faith with the people we know? Your network of friends and acquaintances could be as many as two or three hundred people. There may well be some among that number who are searching for meaning to their life already, and many more could be interested if you started praying for them intentionally. Do you dare? They could be eternally grateful.

In previous chapters we have considered the relationship between three stories in sharing faith: your story, the other person's story, and God's story. These have been corners or points in the triangle of relationships. In the next three chapters we shall look at the three sides and how the people and their stories interconnect.

Let's begin by thinking a little more about the interrelation between 'your story' and 'their story' as indicated by the thick arrows.

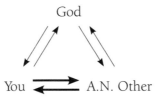

God

You ⇌ A.N. Other

If we want to build relationships and help people respond to God's love, we need to pray for them. Jesus did and so should we. As we shall explore in the parable of the good Samaritan (Luke 10:25–37), we should 'care' for them, too. With prayer and care it is often possible to share with them. Of course, life is not as simple as that, as we shall acknowledge and explore later, but we can start with this as a basic principle.

If we look at how Jesus went about his ministry, it is clear that he used all three ways of operating in no particular order. For him, prayer, care and share were inseparably bound up together. By contrast, we are often relatively good at the praying and brilliant at the caring, but we feel weak in *sharing* the faith explicitly so that other people understand the gospel.

What we shall do in this chapter is:

- Look at our networks and natural connections, our friends and acquaintances.
- Consider what might be good news for the people we know.
- Ask 'Where does God start on the work of salvation?'

Praying for friends and acquaintances

The prayer of a righteous man is powerful and effective.
JAMES 5:16

Eighty per cent of people come to faith through friends and family.
MIKE SPRINGER AND KEVIN HIGHAM [34]

Nearly all the studies I have seen about mission and evangelism seem to show that the main means by which people discover Christian faith is through friendships. The figure of 80 per cent, quoted above, is higher than most, but various research findings illustrate the basic principle. If we are going to dare to share the Christian faith, the people who are most likely to hear it are the people we already know—our friends and acquaintances. Of course, it's brilliant when God calls people to go to places they do not know, like the couple in our church who are currently in Kenya or the retired priest who has just returned from Uganda, but this is not the norm. While there are fantastic opportunities for short-term visits to all kinds of places through project partnerships and mission agencies, most of us spend most of our time in the day-to-day patterns of home and life. That is our 'mission field' where we meet the people we can love and serve.

Just as we pray for those going overseas to serve God, we need to pray for each other. I remember a commissioning service for friends who were going to teach in India. They were invited forward for prayer in front of the congregation, and many Christian friends came to pray and lay hands on them, some of whom teach in inner-city London with a large percentage of Asian children in their classes. It seemed a pity not to commission all the teachers in the congregation!

In addition to praying for each other in the church, we need to pray for the people we know in our wider networks, especially if they don't come to church or call themselves Christian. Prayer is the key factor that affects how, when and where we share faith the Jesus way. My personal view is that the main reason why we do not find ourselves sharing our faith naturally is that we have not been praying for the people we know and care for. Prayer is unpredictable in its outcome but, the more we pray, the more we end up seeing the work of God happen.

Thankfully, we don't have to feel good, prayerful and close to God in order to be used by him. Linda was involved in our church's away day for an Alpha course and went to it saying, 'I am not sure why I am doing this. I feel lousy.' However, in a time of prayer during the day, she laid hands on another person, whose life was completely transformed as a result. God can use us despite ourselves—partly, I think, because God's love sustains us through the times when we feel least like praying. It is one reason why we should relax about sharing our faith and just be prepared to do it. The Holy Spirit does the rest.

I know it is easier to suggest praying than it is to spend time in prayer, but we can be encouraged: Jesus is our example; he prayed and taught us to pray. The Lord's Prayer is a model for our prayer (Matthew 6:9–13). If you don't find it easy to pray in any other ways or for any length of time, try simply saying the Lord's Prayer. After breakfast, my wife Linda and I try to read the New Daylight daily Bible notes from BRF. If time is short, we may just say the Lord's Prayer together. Those brief moments put the rest of the day into perspective.

The great prayer of Jesus sometimes called the 'high priestly prayer' (John 17) shows that he prayed for his disciples and for new believers: 'My prayer is not for them alone. I pray for those who will believe in me through their message, that all of them may be one, Father, just as you are in me and I am in you. May they also be in us so that the world may believe that you have sent me' (John 17:20–21). This prayer is an example to all of us. If Jesus prayed 'for them also', so should we.

Many of us get discouraged in our praying because nothing seems to happen, no matter how hard we pray. Indeed, prayer can feel like a dramatic failure or simply like talking to a brick wall. I suspect that many of us have that experience from time to time. Some of our grandparents have been praying for their family members for decades and not seen them come to a personal commitment and faith in Christ, while other parents have brought up their children as Christians and seen them turn completely against God. We are sometimes more than discouraged: we are baffled. Sometimes we are even shocked, like those praying for a young Christian youth worker employed to share her faith but killed in a road accident at the age of 21.

By contrast, there have been times when prayer has been the key to large numbers of unlikely people deciding to follow Christ. More than 40 years ago, Jackie Pullinger went to work in the notorious 'Walled City' in Hong Kong. Drug barons, gang leaders and hardened criminals came to faith in Christ and a ministry of rehabilitation and caring for addicts developed, as described in her book *Chasing the Dragon*. Jackie makes it clear that this ministry was all inspired and empowered by praying in the Spirit. The famous work of Mother Teresa and her Missionaries of Charity, caring for the poor and dying on the streets of Calcutta, won support from around the world. It was all undergirded by a pattern of daily prayer.

Waves of revival have been sweeping across East Africa, South Korea and Latin America for several decades now. Thousands, if not millions, of new Christians have joined the Church worldwide. Sustained prayer initiatives are frequently cited as the reason for so many conversions. There are similar prayer initiatives in Western Europe, such as the Global Day of Prayer,[35] in which 10,000 Christians come together annually in London, praying each year for the church and revival in our nation.

I have come across stories of large numbers of people coming to Christ in the UK as a result of prayer and peer support. There is, for instance, a congregation at St Thomas Crookes in Sheffield[36] where I have heard that 1200 new Christians have joined the church—mainly young people, new to the faith. The average age of the congregation is 27. Prayer was said to be one of the keys to this life-changing movement.

There is also a congregation in a small village chapel in the Forest of Dean which had dwindled to an unsustainable level. The people were praying, however, and an answer to their prayers came in the form of Viv, a Salvation Army officer who felt that God had called her to start a rural church plant for people who did not go to church. The two prayer intentions came together and now 200 people—from the elderly to the children in the Kids' Club—are involved in multiple congregations and engaged in a host of community activities. Viv says that 80 per cent of these people were unchurched four years ago. While we do not have hundreds of 'Viv's to go around, I believe there would be many more such dramatic stories if we really prayed and acted as Jesus did.

Follow-up activities

- This is a three-minute exercise that could shape your prayers for your friends and acquaintances. Take a blank piece of paper and write your name in the centre. The idea is to represent your networks in life in a 'spider diagram' or 'mind map', to help you pray. Systematically write down categories of people you know—for example, friends, colleagues, family and neighbours—and then add names under each heading. The mind map will be a visual reminder of people to pray for.
- Alternatively, start a prayer diary, with a list of different names to pray for on each day of the week. On a Monday, it

might be colleagues, Tuesday might be for family, Wednesday for 'neighbours', and so on.

- Here is a visual aid to prayer, using your hand. The thumb, being close to your body, is a reminder to pray for the people closest to you. The first, or pointing finger is for all those church leaders who have gone ahead to preach, teach, heal and serve, at home and overseas. They are pointing the way. The middle, tallest finger is for the 'important' people you have heard about who have major responsibilities, especially if they are in the news. The ring finger is for relationships: parents, friends, families and children. This finger is also the weakest, so pray for the people you know who are struggling most. The smallest finger is a reminder to pray for your own needs. Remember, in all of this, to think and pray more for people on the edge of or beyond the current network of Christians you know.

- This is a fun group exercise to help Christians to gain confidence in saying something about their faith. I have used it with Church Army students at Speakers' Corner in Hyde Park. Collect some household objects. It does not matter what they are, but you need two items per person. Display them on a tray or small table so that everyone can see them. If you are the leader, introduce the exercise by saying, 'Jesus used all sorts of ordinary objects to say something about the gospel—salt, light, yeast or corn, for example. Here are some everyday things that might have something to teach us about the Christian faith.' Hand an object to a member of the group and ask them to give an impromptu mini-sermon on what that object could illustrate about the gospel message. Items like a torch, pen or tea towel have obvious applications, so try to have some more difficult options to add to the challenge.

Good news for people you know?

'The Spirit of the Lord is upon me, because he has anointed me to preach good news to the poor. He has sent me to proclaim freedom for the prisoners and recovery of sight to the blind, to release the oppressed, to proclaim the year of the Lord's favour.'
LUKE 4:18–19

Before, during and after any contact with Christians and the church, the main thing people want to feel is loved. This is the Jesus way. Sadly, I know of plenty of examples (and you probably do, too) of keen Christians who have failed to see the needs of others, treated people of other religions as less than human, dismissed or been rude to anybody who does not agree with them, and lost interest when an immediate response to the gospel is not forthcoming. The discussion board on a major evangelistic website was taken down because of abusive language and comment, not by atheists or agnostics but by critical Christians.

On the promotional video for Hope 08, Joel Edwards said, 'What the world needs to see is not one million pointing fingers but two million open arms.' Love is not just the first element of the gospel but the whole essence of the good news.

As we have already seen, true love is not doing what

people want so much as seeing their true needs and doing what we can to help. As Christians, caring should be part of our spiritual DNA. Love is the key to the gospel message, from the Ten Commandments in the Old Testament (Exodus 20:1–17) to Jesus' affirmation of the 'greatest commandment' in the New Testament (Mark 12:28–34; Matthew 22:34–40) and his command in John 15:12–13: 'Love each other as I have loved you. Greater love has no one than this, that he lay down his life for his friends.' Paul reminds us, in 1 Corinthians 13, that love is the greatest gift. The only 'good news' that many people are likely to see is love; our task is not to force but to love people into God's kingdom.

Love is fundamental to evangelism but it is very easy for it to be ignored or taken for granted. Let's think now about some ways in which we can show love and care for the people we know.

Prayer

The first is through prayer. I make no apologies for returning to prayer again, but this time we will consider prayer not as our personal intercessions but as something we offer to people as a way of showing the love and care that are fundamental to the good news.

Some surveys show an increase in interest in spirituality outside the church, and we can reconnect with this interest. In the BBC Millennium survey 'The Soul of Britain', it was found that '76 per cent of people admit to having had a spiritual or religious experience of some kind'.[37] When Christian groups go to festivals, set up a tent and offer prayer in the name of Jesus, queues form as people reach out for some kind of care or blessing, even if they have no understanding of its source. By offering to pray for them, we are connecting with that hunger and connecting them with God.

Praying for people is good news. People are almost universally pleased if you say you are going to pray for them, either as an individual or as a church. From my experience, I can think of only one occasion when someone said that they did not want prayer: their response was, 'Well, you can if you like'—and they had a Christian faith!

Outside the church context, I have heard of business meetings starting with a reflection and space to be silent to collect thoughts. I know of a group of postgraduate scientists who were taken on a 'retreat' paid for by their research company. Meditation evening classes often have a waiting list. People are hungry for something spiritual. As part of a long faith-sharing weekend, we did some street visiting and invited prayer requests that would be included in the prayers at a special service and by Christians forming a 'chain of prayer'. People started to talk about all sorts of personal problems on the doorstep, as they appreciated the offer and the visit.

Church

The second aspect of 'good news' that people often appreciate finding out about, even if they do not attend, is church. While there are some amazing churches 'for the unchurched',[38] including 'Fresh Expressions' and 'emerging church' for people new to faith, 'traditional' or 'inherited' church still connects with a surprisingly large percentage of the population. A survey for English Heritage in 2003 found that 40 per cent of the population in UK urban cities said they visited church buildings as 'spiritual places'.[39] The National Churches Trust also quotes research suggesting that 86 per cent of the population have visited a place of worship within the last twelve months.[40] This is an astonishing counterbalance to the message we usually hear about falling attendance figures.

A recent initiative to invite people to revisit church illustrates just how much public worship is still 'good news' for people today. Back to Church Sunday is a simple initiative in which friends and acquaintances are invited to come along to church. In 2009, 4650 churches in the UK were involved and 80,000 people accepted the invitation, with the long-term result that 10,000 people became new churchgoers.[41] In 2006, Tearfund produced a report called *Churchgoing in the UK* and found that 7.6 million adults in the UK go to church. Further to that (and a huge surprise for many church leaders), another 3 million are waiting to be invited![42]

It goes without saying that what the church offers, like the gospel itself, is multi-faceted. As well as Sunday worship, friendship and space for reflection, many churches offer children's and young people's activities, lunch clubs, social events, even sports and leisure activities—not to mention schools, halls and a host of charitable foundations. The church is brilliant at maintaining a 'service industry' that provides the equivalent of millions of pounds in voluntary work done each year. A university recently researched churches in one county and found that, if calculated at £10 per hour, the voluntary hours given by church members would be valued at £1.39million per year. Christians volunteer in care services outside the church, too, in a vast array of diverse initiatives from hospital transport to foster care, youth mentoring and care-home visiting. Whether it is the church gathered or the church scattered, this is all part of what the Christian community offers in the name of Christ.

Experience

The third aspect of the good news that connects with people, their needs and their interest in something spiritual is an experience. One reason for inviting people to church is that they might have a good experience of God and his people, but of course you don't have to be in a church building to be with God's people. There is probably no better way of getting a chance to chat about faith than going away together. From a church walk to a longer pilgrimage, a concert, a weekend house party, an activity camp or retreat, a conference or a festival, the list of possibilities is endless.

One straightforward way to do this is to take someone to an event or series of events where the gospel will be explained, like an Alpha or Christianity Explored[43] course, or Just 10,[44] which relates the gospel to issues in life illustrated by the Ten Commandments. In your networks of churches, there is likely to be an opportunity for this sort of event somewhere, even if your own congregation does not have the capacity to run one.

If we listen to a number of faith journey stories, it often emerges that we need more opportunities for people to hear a speaker. One of the easiest ways is to invite people to a social event, whether a breakfast or a barbecue. As with everything in church, when such an event is planned, we must have an eye for the needs of other people rather than ourselves. The first miracle of Jesus was at a social event (John 2:1–12) and we do well to provide a variety of such occasions, to which we can invite people of all ages and backgrounds. Social events afford the opportunity to say why we believe, and to name the name of Jesus. Faith journey stories often describe people getting involved in a church before committing their lives to Christ, through a series of such events, often over a number of years. Frequently, people belong before they believe.

Another possibility is a musical concert or a performance of drama, dance or other art form. These events can often explore the Christian faith more explicitly than can a pub quiz or party. A striking example is the ancient tradition of the passion play—a retelling of the events of Jesus' last hours. One production involving various churches, a college, the BBC and the regular Army in Winchester was produced by Howard Mellor (then minister at The United Church, Winchester). He described it as a parable, which is 'an experience, rather than a set of formulae which have to be learned'.

Asking questions

Another way of connecting the good news of Jesus with the interests and needs of people you know is to provide opportunities for them to ask questions about the big issues in life. Even Christians can be tempted to sweep important issues under the carpet, and every church should have some facility for people to ask questions, raise doubts and find support. Even the tiniest rural church is in a network where this can happen. I have already mentioned enquirer courses, but I am also thinking of discussion groups and book clubs, film nights and pub events. You could have a 'hot potato' night (baked potato followed by exploration of a 'hot potato' question) or a Pints of View[45] quiz and discussion night. A growing number of churches have a regular café church[46] event with live music, where discussion becomes natural in a café atmosphere.

Listening is probably the most forgotten tool in the evangelism toolkit. Let's consider the six biggest questions your friends and acquaintances are likely to ask, drawing on information from research in Coventry.[47]

1. Destiny: what happens after we die?
2. Purpose: why are we here?
3. The universe: accident or design?
4. Is there a God?
5. What about the supernatural?
6. Why is there so much suffering?

A group of students at Southampton University recently started collecting and answering the questions that other students asked about Christianity. On Facebook you can see an amazing list of 700–800 questions that have already been asked by students about the Christian faith, from an initiative called 'Text a Toastie'.[48]

Paul, a student involved in this initiative, tells the story:

A video on Facebook describes how, on Wednesday nights in term time between 8pm and midnight, any student at the university can text in for a toastie of their chosen flavour from four options. The toastie is free and delivered to their door if they ask a question about the Christian faith. Members of the Christian Union are ready in various locations to receive the message, make the toastie and cycle off with it wrapped in foil, ready to hand over the toastie and a brief answer to the question. Around 30 volunteers respond to an average of 100 texts a week.

Paul says that responses have been 'very good'. Thirty per cent of the people who text want the free food, listen to the answer but don't develop the conversation. Around 20–30 per cent become more engaged and have a brief conversation, while another 30 per cent are ready for a half-hour conversation about the Christian faith.

With this story in mind, let's think about the parable of the good Samaritan (Luke 10:25–37), as it reminds us to 'care'.

The story Jesus told is perfectly crafted. The two people who might have been expected to help the man who was left for dead walked by on the other side (vv. 31–32), while the despised Samaritan went out of his way and assisted. Not only did he stop to look but he also bandaged the man's wounds, put the man on his own donkey, took him to an inn, stayed overnight, paid for the care and promised to pay more money if it was needed. What a hero! Jesus is very clear in his criticism and praise, and these may well have been shocking words to the people who first heard them.

Here are some questions to consider:

- What was the initial question put to Jesus (v. 25)?
- Why did Jesus give the teacher of the law this particular answer?

- How did this story fit into a dialogue or conversation?
- What else can we learn about sharing faith the Jesus way from this passage?

The teacher of the law was one of two people who asked Jesus the same question: 'What must I do to inherit eternal life?' He got a very surprising answer. If someone asked me the same question, I would be more likely to work through the 'ABC' of salvation (see Chapter 5), but, as we have seen before, Jesus knew the man's particular need and spoke directly to it.

In considering needs, it is worth noting what is often called 'Maslow's hierarchy of needs'. The American psychologist Abraham Maslow identified a hierarchy of basic and not-so-basic needs that have to be met before we can reach our potential in life. The physiological needs of food, warmth, sleep and so on are the most basic. Once they have been satisfied, the next level of need is to do with safety. If this need is met, we are then in a position to meet our social need for friends and companionship. A higher level still relates to esteem: we need to feel 'worthwhile'. The highest level of all is 'self-actualisation'—in other words, 'fulfilling potential'. This analysis is directly relevant to the gospel because we can see how Jesus met needs at all these levels, both with his disciples and with individuals he encountered, from the hungry being fed (Matthew 14:13–21) to the sinner being forgiven (Luke 5:17–26). Look again at the story of the woman at the well (John 4) with Maslow's hierarchy in mind, for example.

Follow-up activities

- Think of your own social networks again. Think of the individuals you have been praying for and the needs that some of them have. Now think of your church fellowship and the ways in which it can be good news for the people you know. Think of events, festivals, conferences, courses or other resources that could be helpful in meeting the spiritual interest of your friends and acquaintances.

- Try visiting your nearest bookshop to see what books, DVDs or other resources could be made available to you and your friends to discuss aspects of the Christian faith. Bible Society has two initiatives that may help: *Reel Issues* provides examples of discussion material based on film clips, while *Lyfe* has stylish Bible-related material for café style discussion.[49]

- We have been thinking about 'good news for the people you know'. Think about how you know people, especially in the virtual and social networking sites on the internet. How does all of the above relate in this context? What do we mean by 'community' these days? If Facebook was a country, it would apparently be the fourth largest in the world. Spend some time thinking and praying about sharing faith the Jesus way online with the people you know.

Where does God start on the work of salvation?

The seed on good soil stands for those with a noble and good heart, who hear the word, retain it, and by perseverance produce a crop.
LUKE 8:15

In the Introduction, I quoted a short devotional passage that dramatically changed my understanding of the gospel, faith-sharing and evangelism many years ago. It led me to write the study booklet *The 360 Gospel of Jesus*[50] and develop the website www.jesus360.org.uk, which accompany this book. I think it is such an important quote that I am repeating it here:

An essentially biblical emphasis—all too often ignored by the church—is that Christ is Lord and Saviour of the whole of a person, or he is no saviour at all. Because Jesus insisted on seeing the person whole, one could never be sure which aspect of a person's need he would tackle first. Here comes the paralysed man, helpless and obviously sick in body. His friends have bought him hoping for a simple cure, and Jesus talks about the forgiveness of sins. Here on the other hand comes a clear case of spiritual need, an enquirer asking how to gain eternal life, and Jesus gives him an economic answer, telling him how to give away his goods to the poor. Because ultimately Jesus cannot rest content until all of a person's needs are fully met, it does not matter much to him where he starts on the work of salvation.[51]

Although this will be a challenge to some who think there is only one way to preach the gospel, it encapsulates an approach that opens many more doors for people to hear the good news.

There are many church leaders, evangelists and theologians who suggest a single way to be a Christian. As we have already discussed, some preach the same message to everyone— 'You must be born again' (John 3:3)—and infer that no other message is sufficient for salvation. Some Christians in the Pentecostal tradition look for evidence that a person is saved in whether or not they speak in tongues (described in 1 Corinthians 14). In other traditions, church membership is the critical factor: both Saint Cyprian in the Catholic tradition and John Calvin in the Reformed tradition wrote along these lines: 'Outside the church there is no salvation.' In other church traditions, baptism is critical—and then there is a debate as to whether infants as well as adults can be baptised. As you can see, there is an ongoing discussion among Christians as to what actually constitutes being a Christian! At the risk of sounding over-simplistic, I would say that all these issues are like the facets of the diamond that we considered earlier. They are different but equally important ways of looking at the same thing—following Christ.

Jesus teaches, shows and provides us with the way of salvation. In that sense, simply 'being a follower of Jesus' is sufficient: it was all that was needed in his day. The thief on the cross was only hours from death when Jesus said to him, 'I tell you the truth, today you will be with me in paradise' (Luke 23:43).

We have seen that Jesus had a different word, action, miracle or healing for each person who came to him. Interestingly, though, healing, wholeness and salvation all find their root in the same Greek word: *sozo*. In essence, they are all interconnected, and Jesus was interested in seeing the person 'whole' and in a 'right relationship' with God. This was what mattered most to him.

The simple answer to the question, 'Does it matter where God starts on the work of salvation?' is 'No'. In his infinite wisdom, God knows what need has to be addressed first. Here is a surprising story, told by the mother of a student who had not been to church for a long time.

The physics he's studying at university is proving to be so absolutely amazing, and showing things to be so perfectly designed and in total relationship with each other, that he's becoming convinced that there must be a God behind it all. He's genuinely awestruck about what he is learning. Tim said that he might not go to church any more, but his study of physics is where he feels he is learning about God at the moment.

Remember Bob, whom we read about earlier? For him, 'it all started with a toaster'.

Benita Hewitt of Christian Research has read many faith journey stories and observes the variety of starting points, from the mundane to the once-in-a-lifetime. They include washing hair, having a child, moving house and bereavement, to name just four. Many of us can look back at a number of possible starting points. When I stop and think about my own faith journey, I can count nine 'starting points' or significant stepping stones along the way.

Have another look at your own faith journey and think about the starting point. Was there just one or were there many? Ask a few friends from your church to share their stories and starting points. It would be interesting to know what the average number of 'starting points' was for a group of Christians from diverse backgrounds.

A survey by Christian Research, based on 207 stories from people of all ages and across all church traditions, threw up some interesting facts:

- Christians in the 55–64 age group are more likely than others to have come to faith suddenly rather than gradually.
- For those who became a Christian suddenly, the average age at which it happened was 20.
- For those who became a Christian gradually, the average age at which it started happening was 13.
- For those who became a Christian gradually, it took place over six to eight years on average.
- 36 per cent of Christians say that, as adults, they have been encouraged in their faith journey.by a dream or vision.
- 50 per cent of Christians were encouraged in their faith journey when young by a Christian friend.
- As adult Christians, 45 per cent say that their faith was encouraged by parents, while 16 per cent say they were discouraged by parents.
- For Christians who had experienced bereavement, 75 per cent said it had had no influence on their faith journeys, but 20 per cent said it had had a positive influence.

- The average age at which young Christians first started to be strongly encouraged by a friend was just before 13.
- The first strongly encouraging influence on a Christian's faith is usually parents, beginning at about the age of six.

The last research finding is interesting. Francis Xavier, who dedicated himself as a Jesuit in 1534, was a great pioneer for the gospel and is often quoted as saying, 'Give me a child for his first seven years and I'll give you the man.' Do we invest in children's work? We should do so, not just because these children will become adult members of the church one day, but because they can be Christians now. It is wrong to think, 'They will be part of the church tomorrow': they should be 'part of the church today'.

The Christian Research survey results suggest that of all the activities of the church, children's work is probably the most important. As Jesus said, 'Whoever welcomes one of these little children in my name welcomes me; and whoever welcomes me does not welcome me but the one who sent me' (Mark 9:37).

One church recognised this and decided to start a children's church after school on a Tuesday, because in that community most children were not free on a Sunday. Lasting less than an hour, everything in the session was geared to the level of children, including the administration of Holy Communion. The children loved it and the parents loved it, too. To some of the parents, it was 'proper' church. Now there were two congregations, on Tuesday and on Sunday. The minister likes to make the point that the first time the two congregations came together was on Christmas Eve. It happened to fall on a Tuesday that year, so the adults went to Children's Church!

Perhaps the next most significant age group for the church is the 'baby-boomers'. According to the research, those in the 55- to 64-year-old age bracket are most likely to have sudden conversions. Graham Horsley was the evangelism adviser for the Methodist Church when he said, 'I think the baby-boomer generation are the most open dechurched group of people that we have in Britain today. They are the ones most reachable as they have some vestige of Christian teaching from being a child and they are wondering what life is going to be like in the future.'

Having considered how we can help people make a start on their faith journey, in the next chapter we shall look at how we encourage them to grow into mature disciples of Christ.

Follow-up activities

- Consider the Christian Research findings with your friends and ask if the survey results reflect your own experience among the Christians you know.
- Think of the children's work in your church and consider the motivation behind it. Is it intended to produce adult members later or to help children become alive to the Christian faith now?
- Now think of the people you know in the 55- to 64-year-old group who are not linked in with church. From what you have read so far, is there a way of connecting with them that could lead to discussions of faith?

Chapter 5

Accompany those who follow Jesus

The next day Jesus decided to leave for Galilee. Finding Philip, he said to him, 'Follow me.' Philip, like Andrew and Peter, was from the town of Bethsaida. Philip found Nathanael and told him, 'We have found the one Moses wrote about in the Law, and about whom the prophets also wrote—Jesus of Nazareth, the son of Joseph.' 'Nazareth! Can anything good come from there?' Nathanael asked. 'Come and see,' said Philip.

JOHN 1:43–46

Philip did a beautiful, profound and life-changing thing: he brought Nathanael to Jesus. As a result, he is sometimes described as 'the first evangelist'. In another sense, he was a coach or mentor: he encouraged Nathanael and helped him to find faith.

Coaching and mentoring are words given to the process of helping, encouraging and equipping people to reach their potential. We are well used to teachers and tutors having this role in education, and ministers and pastors exercising this ministry in the church. Nowadays, new colleagues at work often have an induction course and a 'buddy up' system so that they quickly learn everything from where to make a cup of coffee to how to process accounts correctly.

In the same way that Philip brought Nathanael to Jesus, so we are to bring people to Jesus in our day, helping them in their first steps of following him. We might do this in conversations, meetings, phone calls, the odd text, online or in a group discussion, at church or on an enquirers' course. We can mentor by just spending time with a new Christian, or by specifically praying or discussing a book, film or Bible passage on a regular basis—for example, once a week for a month. Listening is the key, but we can also share leisure activities, going with them to their events, as well as taking them to ours on a longer-term basis.

There are two key Bible passages for this chapter. The first is the call of the fishermen (Mark 1:16–20; Matthew 4:18–22) and the second is the appearance of Jesus to the disciples on the road to Emmaus (Luke 24:13–35). These passages illustrate how Jesus walked with the disciples, helping them to understand along the way, at both the beginning and the end of their faith journeys. Jesus was an accompanier.

In this chapter we shall consider:

• Helping friends as they take their first steps on the faith journey
• How we accompany them 'side by side' on their journey
• Stepping stones to help them become mature disciples of Jesus

Remembering the triangle of relationships between us, our friends and God, in this chapter we shall think about how their story connects with God's story.

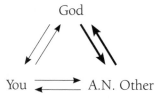

First steps on the faith journey

Coaching is a thoroughly biblical process. Throughout the Old and New Testaments there are repeated examples of key relationships where one person draws alongside another to help them achieve their potential: Jethro advising Moses, Elisha learning from Elijah, Jesus teaching his disciples, Barnabas encourages first Saul and then Mark.

BOB HOPKINS AND FREDDY HEDLEY[52]

As we have seen, studies on lots of faith journeys suggest that people go through various stages as they first come to faith and then grow in Christ. At this point, we shall consider one of these studies as it relates to people responding to God's love from a position completely outside the church and with no previous knowledge of the Christian faith at all.

Although it's a simple diagram to illustrate a far more complex journey, over the years I have found the 'Engel scale' a very helpful tool. Adapted in many different forms over the years, it reminds me that the whole Christian life is a journey and our role is to encourage everyone along it. The order of the steps may be different for each individual but the overall principle is a helpful reminder of how the journey may often unfold. The steps start at -10 and reach '0' at the point when someone chooses to become a disciple of Jesus. In the later stages, numbers are dispensed with as the stages vary so much, depending on the individual.

-10 Awareness of the supernatural
-9   No effective knowledge of Christianity
-8   Initial awareness of Christianity
-7   Interest in Christianity
-6   Awareness of basic facts of the gospel
-5   Grasp of implications of the gospel
-4   Positive attitude to the gospel
-3   Awareness of personal need
-2   Challenge and decision to act
-1   Repentance and faith
 0   A disciple is born
+1   Evaluation of decision
+2   Initiation into the church
+3   Becoming part of the process of making other disciples
+4   Growth in understanding of the faith
+5   Growth in Christian character
-    Discovery and use of gifts
-    Christian lifestyle
-    Stewardship of resources
-    Prayer
-    Openness to others/Effective sharing of faith and life[53]

Laurence Singlehurst has written about the Engel scale in *Sowing Reaping Keeping*,[54] using the analogy of sowing for the harvest described in John 4:34–38. We are 'sowing' the seeds of the gospel when we help people take the early steps of faith, 'reaping' when we help them make their own personal commitment, and 'keeping' when we help them continue to grow as Christians.

Think of anyone whom you are accompanying at the start of their faith journey. How many of the stages above have they passed through in the time you have known them?

When Jesus called the fishermen to follow him (see Mark 1:16–20), he said, 'Come, follow me, and I will make you fishers of men' (v. 17). He was offering to show them by example, as a craftsman would train an apprentice. He was offering himself as a buddy, accompanier, coach or mentor as we would understand the role today. Jesus walked many miles with these men, eating the same meals, sleeping in the same places, visiting the same people, discussing what was happening, sailing in the same boat and sharing many other activities as they spent three years on the road together. The disciples saw what Jesus did, heard what Jesus said and followed what Jesus instructed as they went where Jesus went.

At the end of the three years together, after the death of Jesus, two of his wider group of disciples (not among the Twelve) were walking along the road to Emmaus, about seven miles from Jerusalem, when 'Jesus himself came up and walked along with them' (Luke 24:15). This is a picture of how Jesus treated his followers—with a combination of gentleness and authority, so that, as they walked with him, these disciples discovered and understood the truth of what had been happening and heard what he had to say about it all.

Both of these passages show us that Jesus accompanies those who follow him. Whether he spent a lot of time with his close friends or had a brief encounter with someone in the street, like the woman who touched his cloak (Luke 8:42b–48), we see Jesus giving time, in making conversation, revealing truth and doing the work of God.

You might not spend that amount of time with your friends and acquaintances, but it is quite possible that as you pray, you become a spiritual guide to friends wanting to find out more about the Christian faith. You may not even recognise that this is happening. If you do, and patterns emerge, you might agree to meet regularly, discuss issues together, pray and encourage each other. You could even find that a small group of people comes together and the meeting becomes a regular event at a local coffee shop. This might sound surprising but it has happened in all sorts of places. Remember me mentioning café churches? This is often how they have started.

Seeing people grow in faith can be a real adventure for them and for you. Don't be too surprised if they ask you lots of questions and do all the running. Alternatively, don't be disappointed if they seem interested and then nothing more happens—or, indeed, if they show no interest at all.

Just keep praying. It is strange how unpredictable the process can be. Often, a new Christian is so enthusiastic about the faith they have discovered that they set the agenda: they will be phoning you and asking questions. In turn, they may become instant evangelists. Like the newly converted apostle Paul, many new Christians will be asking, 'What shall I do, Lord?' (Acts 22:10). It's a dangerous question: we have no idea where it might lead us!

The key is to think, as we have already done in considering the Jesus way, about what is most helpful for the other person. We must remember that it is more important, especially in the early days of faith, to help people on their own terms. Later on, this approach may need to be balanced with the needs of the wider Christian fellowship, but for now, the place to start is with the individual.

It may be that 'church' is the greatest resource you have to help a new Christian grow. Through church, the new believer can find worship, encouragement, teaching, support and resources for their journey. Therefore, all churches should have some way of making people feel welcome. This may mean simply saying 'hello' at the door, but it can also involve thinking about who else to introduce to the new person. Of course, some people like to be anonymous when they go to church and may prefer big congregations so they can remain more private in their prayer. Always keep in mind the importance of helping visitors to feel respected and welcome. See the resources in Appendix B for more information.

However, 'starting where they are' may mean that church, even though it is wonderful to you, might not be the most helpful next step for other people as they start to follow

Christ. There could be a wide variety of reasons for this. People who have completed an Alpha course together, for example, have often found that they like to stay together as a group. People for whom English is not their first language might also like to meet with others who share their cultural background. Many people who have not been involved in church may be at work on a Sunday or have commitments to do with their hobbies or families.

Here is a slight twist. When we look at Jesus, we can end up feeling quite challenged by our own involvement in church, important though it is for our own growth and fellowship, and because it provides much for new Christians, too. In the Gospels, we see that Jesus spent very little time in the equivalent of church! Although he described the temple as 'my Father's house' (Luke 2:49; John 2:16) and he read the scriptures in the synagogue (Luke 4:16), we don't hear of him visiting either of them on a regular or even irregular basis. As we have seen, his encounters and the faith journeys of his disciples were in everyday situations, not in religious meetings and buildings. Paradoxically, we need to bring more people into church at the same time as some of us need to get out more.

Is this a challenge to you? Do you need to get out of the church more? Is God calling you to get involved in things other than 'church' in order to bring about more of his kingdom?

Graham tells the story of helping young people do outdoor pursuit activities, often at weekends. 'Here,' he says, 'people are naturally open to experience and understand themselves in a new way. After they have achieved something, it is easy to say, "From what you have just experienced, you can see that there is more to life." In one conversation a young lady said, "I thought what I could see around me [the hills] was fantastic, but what I've discovered beneath the surface is even more amazing."' Graham goes on, 'It was a God-given opportunity for me to suggest to her and the others I was talking to how much more there may be to life, beneath the surface and as yet undiscovered—who they really are, why they are here, and what is the purpose of life. This might also turn out to be "even more amazing", too.'

Church Army students thought about where Jesus would be on a Sunday morning. They prayed about it, asked for support and got involved with the local car boot sale. They offered to pray for people, as they had Christian books as well as bric-a-brac for sale—and were surprised by the interest generated.

When we meet for worship, we are the gathered church. When we go about our daily business, we are the scattered church. It is in the wider world that we are to be salt and light (Matthew 5:13–16) and it is here that we can help people take their first steps of faith. Yes, the church is the kingdom community and we need all sorts of people to run it, but how many of us need to be released to get involved in politics, the environment, community activities and the like?

A number of resources have been developed to support people as they start to grow in faith. I have mentioned the

Alpha course, which is probably the most well-known and highly effective, but there are a number of others detailed in Appendix B. I would especially like to highlight the website 'Now a Christian'.[55] This is relatively new and provides an online community of new Christians of all ages, encouraging each other as they follow short readings sent by email. It is commended by Colin, who says:

For somebody who has just come to faith I found the website pitched at just the right level with the language and content. It is good to see the comments from other people in the 'cloud' that comes up from what they have said in the community area. It is a nice program with step-by-step information and suggestions for people new to Christianity. It was just perfect for where I am at the moment.

Follow-up activities

- Consider how you can help people you know to grow in their faith by either bringing them together as a group or enabling them to meet other Christians who could encourage them.
- Consider the ministry of welcome in your home church. Whatever the current arrangements, keep a lookout for the person going unnoticed. Try to make sure the welcome they receive is a helpful and appropriate one.
- If you belong to a discussion group, consider how the principle of 'sowing, reaping, keeping' can be absorbed by members so that you not only grow as a group but also help new people grow with you.

- Finally, either as a group or individually, think about whether you are too much involved in church to be meeting people who do not attend, in order to help them find faith and take first steps in believing.

Side by side on the faith journey

Evangelism is just one beggar telling another beggar where to buy bread.

ATTRIBUTED TO D.T. NILES, QUOTING MARTIN LUTHER

Assuming you are already alongside people who are starting their journey of faith, the question arises: 'What do you say to help people take their first steps on this journey?'

If a friend says to you, 'And what did you do over the weekend?' don't leave out the word 'church' from your answer if that was part of your weekend! I did that recently, as I thought the other person wouldn't be interested. The easiest thing to do is simply to answer a question, without being embarrassed if the answer says something about your Christian faith.

As you get to know people, the depth of conversation naturally changes. Although some people do not like to discuss things at a deeper level, it is sometimes surprising how others will dive straight in. When we get to talk about more personal things, such as what we think about various issues, the values we hold or what motivates us, it is quite natural to talk about faith.

When someone has got to the point of talking about

spiritual matters at a deeper level, I might ask, 'Do you mind me asking if God ever figures in that thinking?' On another occasion it might be right to ask, 'What do you think Jesus would say to that?' If a particular need has become apparent and I think someone would appreciate prayer, I often find it easy to say, 'I'd love to pray with you about that.' Of course you can't force the conversation, but the right word in the right place can open all sorts of doors and may be much appreciated by the other person. While such conversations may seem easier for those of us in full-time church work, they are possible for all Christians everywhere. Often it is a case of having the confidence as much as the opportunity, and the more you are comfortable talking about your faith to Christian friends, the more able you will be to share it with everyone else.

It is always a good idea to have stories in mind, not just from your own faith journey but also from the experiences of other Christians. Statements sound dogmatic and loaded, but stories can be much more effective at conveying truth: they are also easier to listen to. Jesus often told stories and they were a central part of his way of sharing faith. The key is not to make them too long and to leave people wanting more.

We have already thought about the importance of dialogue in sharing the Christian faith, but it is easy to forget that dialogue includes disagreement. There would be no conversation if we agreed with each other all the time. I often find myself saying, 'I understand that but have a completely different view.' This continues the discussion and makes it more interesting—and is creative, as long as I listen and engage with the other person's point of view too.

Christians do not have the right to be right all the time.

We should always be open to the possibility of changing our minds. Surprisingly, even Jesus changed his mind. He was on the road with his disciples when a Canaanite woman cried out for him to release her demon-possessed daughter. Amazingly, she acknowledged him as 'Lord, Son of David', and he said nothing, even though she had asked for mercy. The disciples suggested that Jesus should send her away, and Jesus seemed to agree with their words, saying, 'I was sent only to the lost sheep of Israel'. It appears that the woman had to stop Jesus from continuing on his way by kneeling before him. For a second time, she acknowledged him as 'Lord' and begged for help. This time, Jesus seemingly insulted her by suggesting that the 'children's bread should not be given to dogs'. She was undeterred, though, and came back at Jesus a third time, whereupon he finally changed his mind, as if to say 'Fair enough!' You can read about this dramatic encounter in Matthew 15:21–28.

One way of preparing for conversation and dialogue is to sit down for five minutes with a Bible and your journal (if you have one), and ask yourself, 'Which passage about Jesus means most to me at the moment?' Then read it and note three things that speak to you from it. This passage is part of God's story and, if it is part of your story too, it could be relevant to your friends' stories. It's worth considering whether you could read this passage along with your friend. Having said that, as well as sharing what it means to you, it is vital to listen to what it means to the other person, too.

Although people don't like to be talked at, sometimes there will be a point at which they say, 'Explain it to me, then.' This is not the time to tell your story so much as to offer a simple explanation of the basics of the Christian faith. If they are asking, in effect, 'How do I become a Christian?' you could have one or more well-known Bible texts to hand (see below). Quoting sentences of scripture was part of the armoury Jesus used against the devil during the temptation in the wilderness (Luke 4:1–13). However, because quoting the scripture can have a dramatic effect, I think we have to be careful how and when we quote the Bible to people who are not familiar with it. It is interesting that Jesus did not use this approach very often, and today, diving straight into the Bible can even stop people hearing the very news we are trying to share. We need to discern the right quote and a timely moment to share these powerful words.

Here are some of the best-known verses:

- 'God so loved the world that he gave his one and only Son, that whoever believes in him shall not perish but have eternal life' (John 3:16). This is sometimes called the 'gospel in a nutshell'.
- 'Here I am! I stand at the door and knock. If anyone hears my voice and opens the door, I will come in and eat with him, and he with me' (Revelation 3:20). This verse is often linked to the painting *Jesus the Light of the World* by Holman Hunt, with the observation that the door does not have a handle on Jesus' side: he waits for us to open the door. (Remember that the context of this text is actually about the church as well as individuals.)

- 'Righteousness from God comes from faith in Jesus Christ
  to all who believe. There is no difference, for all have
  sinned and fall short of the glory of God, and are justified
  freely by his grace through the redemption that came by
  Jesus Christ' (Romans 3:22–24). I have found that these
  verses are best read from the page rather than quoted in
  conversation—partly because the passage is long but also
  because people are much more likely to see the significance
  if they read it for themselves.

Another approach is not to quote scripture but to share a
personal conviction. People are often interested in what
motivates others. This is not quite the same as sharing a faith
story. What I do is to explain which core parts of the gospel
story make particular sense to me; it is my own conviction:

*For me, it all comes down to the resurrection. The Roman histor-
ians recorded the person and crucifixion of Jesus, so it must have
happened in history, whether you believe in the Bible or not. But
there is no burial place for us to visit. The followers not only say
they saw him alive after three days but their lives were transformed.
Instead of disappearing, they spoke publicly with great power and
authority, despite being in fear for their lives. They were absolutely
sure Jesus was alive. If the resurrection really happened, then it
changes everything!*

Another way of explaining something of the gospel message
is to use a diagram. Several examples have been used over the
years and you will find them in books about evangelism. The
model I have used here is the triangle and the interconnection

of three relationships: you, the other person and God. The gospel is all about relationships, so I have used the triangle as a diagram to show God's love for us all and the invitation he holds out to us to respond and have a relationship in Christ. All diagrams have their limitations but I have found this one to be helpful as part of a conversation about the Christian faith.

Although I have said that Jesus did not use a formula, at the same time it can be helpful to other people if we have a thought-out, straightforward framework for explaining the first steps of the Christian faith journey. People are used to working with acronyms, lists, memorable phrases and head-lines. I find the 'ABC' explanation helpful and memorable. These are headlines that can act as a starting point for further conversation.

- Accept that God loves you as you are.
- Believe that Jesus died on the cross for the forgiveness of sin.
- Commit your life to Christ and follow him.

Remember the importance of leaving people wanting to know more: Jesus did!

All the way through this book, I have kept returning to the importance of praying for people. A point comes, however, when it is better to pray with them. Just as helping people to read the Bible for themselves is an important step forward, so helping people to pray themselves is also foundational to their new faith journey. The next thing to think about is how you might help them do it.

When the time is right, and if you feel comfortable praying for people out loud, say that you would love to pray with them. Your prayer can be about the things you have discussed or the particular concerns that the other person has in mind. It may even be that the person wants to follow Christ and you can help them pray for that relationship to be real. A number of resources provide a suggested prayer, often following a pattern that includes the key themes of 'sorry, please and thank you'. Here is an example:

Lord, thank you that you love me.
Thank you that you accept me.
Thank you for dying on the cross for me.
I am sorry for the things I have done wrong.
For the sin I need to say sorry for,
please forgive me,
and help me love you
as I commit my life to you
in Jesus' name.
Amen

Another approach is to say the prayer together that Jesus himself taught us. The Lord's Prayer (Matthew 6:9–13) is the pattern for our prayer. It goes without saying that in helping people take their first steps as a disciple of Jesus, sometimes there can be no better prayer than the one Jesus taught us. When someone is at the point of wanting to follow Christ, especially if they are older and the words of the Lord's Prayer are fairly familiar, it can be an amazing experience to pray the words while reflecting about their personal significance for the first time.

Think about the various approaches outlined above. Have you found any of them helpful in conversations so far with the people you know? Have you used another approach in helping people explore the Christian faith for themselves? How does 'explaining' the gospel fit with 'living' the gospel in your experience?

Earlier, we established that a fundamental aspect of the Jesus way is that Jesus said and did different things for different people, as he perceived their deepest need. It is therefore important to note that no one approach is more important than another. Although the above illustrations have been helpful, none is prescriptive for all Christians in all situations: people have found faith in Christ through these routes and many more. This cannot be emphasised enough. As always, we should be guided by what is most helpful for the other person, as prompted by the Holy Spirit, as we pray and look to Jesus.

Follow-up activities

- Think of any conversations you have had with someone else about the Christian faith. Make a note of anything said about going on with God, which was either helpful or unhelpful.
- If you did not think of a Bible passage earlier and make some notes on what it means to you, do so now. If you have a friend to discuss this book with, you could both

choose your own passage, jot down your comments and then compare notes.

- List any Bible passages or key texts that you have come across, which specifically illustrate the message of the gospel. If you are in a small group, draw up a list between you. Be open to the ideas of other people if they suggest passages which are not 'classic gospel texts': this is a discussion and confidence exercise, not a test.

- If you are in a group, collect some resources for evangelism and discuss how they are intended to be used. See if any are particularly helpful for your own style and personality. Pray about writing your own resource, especially if it can be linked to your church or locality in some way. One church has produced 'my story' brochures, with an update every month, for example.

- Take a look at the Lord's Prayer and rewrite the key points in your own words as a prayer about personal commitment to Christ.

- Finally, think generally about what resources are available. If you are the church minister, consider what visitors to your church may pick up, or what congregation members can give away. See www.evangelismuk.typepad.com for links to further suggestions and ideas.

Stepping stones for the new follower of Christ

Jesus asked them, 'Who do the crowds say I am? … But what about you?' he asked. 'Who do you say I am?'
LUKE 9:18, 20

In their book *Pathway to Jesus*,[56] Don Everts and Doug Shaupp look at the faith journeys of 2000 people who have made a commitment to Christ from the mid 1990s to the present day. Although this is a study of young students in America, their observations are also helpful in the UK context.

They considered the common factors, or 'thresholds' that people crossed in their journey of faith, and came up with five. There are similarities with the Engel scale considered earlier.

- Trust a Christian
- Become curious
- Open up to change
- Seek after God
- Enter the kingdom

Drawing on the parable of the sower and the seed (Mark 4:1– 20), Everts and Shaupp observe:

The image Jesus paints is full of tension, isn't it? At the same time it underlines the mysterious, uncontrollable nature of conversion (the farmer sleeps and yet the seed grows in ways he can't understand) and the need for work (scattering seeds, harvesting with the sickle). While it affirms the hidden nature of change (it happens at night when no one is looking), it also follows the natural, organic process that change follows (first seed, then stalk, then head, then the crop is ready). The growth of the plant may be mysterious, but it still follows nature. It is organic, and this means that for the seed to become a ripe plant, it will grow in a certain way. This was the lesson our friends were teaching us. Each individual path to faith is a unique mystery, but their collective paths to faith had surprising similarities.[57]

This is an exciting quotation because it clearly illustrates the complexity in faith journeys and the way in which several different things are going on at the same time. If you have been a Christian for as long as you can remember, I hope you can see this in the steps taken by other people who are new to faith. Can you identify key 'stepping stones' for them?

As we have already seen, the parable of the sower is a profoundly important Bible passage in understanding how people come to faith, not least because it suggests that Jesus himself recognised and understood that many people, as we sometimes say, 'fall by the wayside'. We need not be surprised when people who show an initial interest in spiritual issues then move on to other concerns. What is important is that we continue to accept and encourage them, as it is clear from all that we have seen in the Gospels so far that God still loves them. God still has an eternal purpose for the people who do not go as far on their journey of discovery as we would like.

In addition, as we have seen, many people take a long time to come to a living faith in Christ. In the past, some Christians have done enormous damage by putting too much pressure on people to make a decision. If there is one thing we can learn from the apostle Peter, it is that Jesus always gives a second chance. Some research has been done on faith journeys and how long they take, on average. A good example of this sort of study was conducted in 1992, when John Finney wrote *Finding Faith Today*.[58] He discovered that the average time between the start of someone's journey of faith and their public profession of faith in baptism, or an equivalent ceremony, was four and a half years.

Helping people find 'stepping stones' for their faith journey is critically important. Most of the faith journeys I have reported, and those on the *Faith Journeys* website, illustrate a variety of steps that people have taken.

Some Christians take the view that the 'stepping stones' and 'sharing stories' approach is insufficient to help people make an informed decision to follow Christ. They are concerned about the choice we face between heaven and hell and suggest that we need to start the conversation at that point. I appreciate that we do people a disservice if we do not add clarity, but, if we are to start where people are and lead them to Christ, such complex issues are best considered later on in the journey of faith. The exception, of course, is if that is the particular question they come with. We are to build bridges, not burn them.

Perhaps the biggest 'stepping stone' for people today is the concept of 'sin'. Interestingly, these days, people rarely have this concept, so we need to be careful how we approach the topic when sharing faith. Jesus' attitude to the woman caught in adultery (John 8:1–11) is a striking example of how Christians should treat other people. He recognised the woman's sin but did not condemn her. He seemed more concerned to challenge the people who wanted to stone her. Another example is Zacchaeus, the man who climbed a tree in order to see Jesus above the crowd. All Jesus said to him was, 'Zacchaeus, come down immediately. I must stay at your house today' (Luke 19:5). It was not Jesus but the crowds who called him a sinner (v. 7), and it was Zacchaeus himself who offered to pay money back to those whom he had cheated. Afterwards, Jesus said, 'Today salvation has come to this house… For the Son of Man came to seek and to save what was lost' (vv. 9–10), but nowhere do we find him metaphorically pointing an accusing finger at Zacchaeus.

Following on from this observation about how Jesus deals with 'sin', we should also consider Jesus and his message to 'repent and believe'. This is one of the three banner head-lines that Robin Gamble has identified as being central to Jesus' gospel,[59] and we read in Mark 1:15, 'The time has come. The kingdom of God is near. Repent and believe the good news!' This finds an echo in the preaching of the disciples—'They went out and preached that people should repent' (Mark 6:12)—and of Peter after the resurrection: 'Repent and be baptised, every one of you, in the name of Jesus Christ for the forgiveness of your sins' (Acts 2:38). The message is repeated often by Paul—for example: 'Now [God] commands all people everywhere to repent' (Acts 17:30). However, the point I notice in reading all the references to 'repent and believe' is that they are general pronouncements rather than instructions to individuals. The nearest Jesus gets to this approach is with a group, as recorded in Luke 13:1–9. Clearly the various groups take the message individually, but the messages are not directed at individuals on a one-to-one basis.

Look at the Top 50 texts in Appendix A and see how many include the basic core concept preached to the crowds: 'Repent and believe'.

Next consider the texts that focus on the choice between heaven and hell. Read the parable of the sheep and the goats (Matthew 25:31–46) and try to identify the criteria for separating the sheep and the goats.

We have already looked at Nicodemus and his interesting faith journey. What about Peter? When did he first commit to following Jesus? Was it when Jesus asked him to leave his nets and follow him (Matthew 4:20)? Was it when he declared, 'You are the Christ' (16:16)? Perhaps it was not until he was challenged to take on the responsibility to 'feed my lambs' (John 21:15–19). In some Pentecostal traditions, the view would be that it was not until he was filled with the Spirit at Pentecost (Acts 2:1–5). Does it matter whether or not we can identify a specific moment? What does matter is that Peter kept taking steps of faith, even if he faltered.

We should remember that we are all on a journey ourselves and that we are encouraging our friends and neighbours to join us. None of us is perfect and the path is strewn with obstacles. However, Jesus shows the way and we are still invited to 'follow'. We are to accompany and nurture each other as we take steps of faith. Don't be surprised if the new Christian becomes more of an encouragement to you than you think you are to them.

A fairly traditional view of evangelism is that a preacher must invite the audience to 'get up out of your seat' and make a decision to follow Christ. Important though that is (and I personally think we need more opportunities rather than fewer for people to hear the gospel message and respond), it is clear from our thinking about the Jesus way that offering help at any point along someone's journey is also important. Evangelism is a process of nurture and growth as much as a decision and turning point.

Interestingly, when Jesus called people to follow him, he formed a close circle of friends—Peter, James and John—whom he mentored daily. However, also among his disciples were others who remained quite anonymous. I am sure Jesus had his eye on them and worked his purpose out through them, but they seemed less obvious. James son of Alpheus, Thaddeus (Judas son of James) and Simon the Zealot are all disciples about whom we have no words of Jesus recorded in the Gospels. In the same way, we may find ourselves mentoring a small group who become an 'inner circle' while others simply remain those for whom we pray regularly and with whom we have occasional contact.

When we pray and encourage each other, it can be daunting not to have a focus. I find 'stepping stones' helpful as an image as it means I can think of individuals and just pray and encourage them to take the next step. This point may seem obvious, but it can help us avoid the risk of making our prayers too general. Being more specific raises our expectation of how a particular prayer might be answered. On the one hand, I would encourage you to focus your prayers, while on the other I would encourage you not to feel a failure if they are not answered as soon as you ask, or in the way that you had hoped. You may pray for decades and still not have the joy of sharing your faith and leading someone to Christ. You might do the praying and others get the privilege of seeing someone make a decision. As we read in 1 Corinthians 3:6, 'I planted the seed, Apollos watered it, but God made it grow'—and that was the experience of the apostle Paul!

In the first chapter, we reflected on how Jesus accepts us as we are—and he accepts other people as they are, too. It might be a challenge to us, but we are to have the same attitude as he did. Some Christians find it very difficult to think in these terms, struggling to imagine how people of other faiths are trying to live their life for God, for example, or to accept the lifestyle choices of their friends. God's timetable may well be very different from ours, and he may deal with what we consider a pressing issue long after someone has come to be a follower of Jesus. As we saw earlier, there is no 'gold standard' that people have to achieve before they can come to faith. If there were, I guess many Christians would probably fail, too. We should remember Jesus' words about the speck in our brother's eye and the plank in our own (Matthew 7:5). We are to encourage people to take steps of faith without undue expectations beyond longing for whatever Jesus has in store for them.

Even if people flatly refuse to have anything to do with the church or to hear a word about the gospel, God is still with them. He still loves them. We are all sinners in need of repentance: it is just that we have turned to Christ sooner rather than later. God has to be at work in people's lives before they come to faith—otherwise they wouldn't be able to come to faith! So be assured, as you pray for your friends and acquaintances, that God has a plan, even if it doesn't seem obvious. What we have to do is discern what we can say and do to help people discover Jesus, who is already with them. Our task is to help them discover God's love, forgiveness and new life for themselves, and, at the right moment, to help them take the next step.

Follow-up activities

- Think of the friends and acquaintances for whom you are praying, and consider what might be an appropriate stepping stone of faith for each one. Is there a smaller group emerging with whom you can spend more time, like Jesus did with Peter, James and John?
- If you are in a study group, think about how the stepping stone analogy fits with the group. What is the next step for 'sowing, reaping and keeping' new members? How are you mentoring each other?
- If you are a church leader, reflect on the idea of coaching and mentoring and how you can develop natural networks for mutual encouragement. What resources could you provide for them?

Chapter 6

Your journey: going on with God

Jesus said… 'Follow me.'
JOHN 21:19

The most urgent priority is to present the figure and
the message of Jesus in his public ministry, and so to help
foster the growth of a living relationship with him.

POPE BENEDICT XVI[60]

We come to our final chapter, which could have been the
first: sharing faith often comes down to the overflow of our
own relationship with God.

Earlier, I acknowledged that sharing faith is difficult for
many Christians because they don't feel as if they have a faith
to share—or, if they do, that it is not worth sharing. If we
want to help other people find faith in God, we need to be in
a growing relationship with him ourselves. We do not have to
be perfect but we do have to be dependent. The Holy Spirit
does the rest.

A banner over the main door of a local Elim Pentecostal
church makes a good point: 'No perfect people allowed.' With

all our imperfections and lack of faith, we still make ourselves available to share faith the Jesus way. To do so, we need to come back to first principles: God loves us as we are. He wants us to move on, to grow and become more like Jesus. As we follow in the steps of Jesus, he wants others to follow too.

The key passage for this chapter is the reinstatement of Peter, where, after his resurrection, Jesus appears to the disciples and, over breakfast on the beach, says to Peter, 'Feed my sheep' and 'Follow me!' (John 21:15–19), despite Peter's previous denial of Jesus. This amazing event was followed by an even more astonishing experience when Peter was filled with the Holy Spirit (Acts 2:4) and addressed the crowd that had gathered in Jerusalem (Acts 2:4, 14–39). He shared his faith from his own personal experience and relationship with God.

In this chapter we shall consider:

- How our relationship with God can overflow to others.
- How the paradoxes in the gospel can help us.
- How the wind of the Spirit empowers our witness.

We shall use our triangle diagram to look at the final relationship: our story together with God's story, and how it is key to sharing faith the Jesus way.

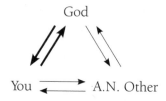

Our relationship with God overflowing

The Lord turned and looked at [Peter]. There is sadness at Peter's failure—Peter who, as ever, had promised so much—but there is continuing love. Jesus is calm where Peter is confused; Jesus is able to see Peter's wretchedness and isolation and he cannot stop loving him; and it this love that is our only hope.
STEPHEN COTTRELL[61]

'Out of the overflow of one's heart the mouth speaks.'
LUKE 6:45

Peter is perhaps the person who best illustrates the Jesus way. He was one of the first fishermen called by Jesus to be a 'fisher of men', one of the inner group of Jesus' closest friends, the one we noted with 'ups' and 'downs' earlier, and the one Jesus addressed with the astonishing words, 'You are Peter, and on this rock I will build my church' (Matthew 16:18). Despite his dramatic denial at the point when Jesus probably needed his friendship most (Matthew 26:69–75; Mark 14:66–72; Luke 22:54–62; John 18:25–27), Peter was reinstated. Jesus appeared to him after the resurrection (Luke 24:34) and personally challenged him with a repeated question: 'Do you truly love me?' (John 21:15, 16, 17). Having had that assurance three times, Jesus finally said to Peter again, 'Follow me!' (v. 19).

Following this reinstatement, the 'power of the Holy Spirit' was probably the last thing Peter expected, yet we read that 'all of them were filled with the Holy Spirit' (Acts 2:4). The experience completely transformed Peter's life in a way that would also change the world. Empowered by the Spirit, he preached in public without fear of what the crowd or the authorities might do to him. He was now on a mission to 'fish for men' in a much bigger sea.

Do you remember, in Chapter 4, my minister's challenge to add the word 'dare' to the list of 'prayer, care and share'? We see in Peter that we don't have to be perfect but we can be empowered by the Holy Spirit to do the work of God. Do we dare to ask for the Holy Spirit to empower us?

Peter's amazing preaching, along with the miracles he performed (for example, Acts 3:1–10), came out of his relationship with God. The same principle is true for us, even if the things we do are not so dramatic, powerful and significant in terms of world history. We make a difference where we are, and it is by the same Holy Spirit, in the name of Jesus, that we too can change the lives of other people. We are not to compare ourselves with Peter and say, 'I have not had a dramatic experience so I cannot do that.' Thank God for those Christians who have done great works, but also thank God for those who have quietly witnessed to their faith and brought others to follow Jesus by the Spirit's ongoing work.

The key, as I see it from reading the Bible, is to be open to whatever God wants to give us. As we have seen, the most basic message from Jesus to his disciples is 'Follow me'. I believe that the Holy Spirit has already done some amazing things with us, but he wants to do much more. Often, it is only after we have stepped out in faith that we realise the Holy Spirit is with us. When Jesus gave the great commission to 'go and make disciples of all nations' (Matthew 28:19), he then gave the reassurance, 'And surely I am with you always, to the very end of the age' (v. 20).

Do you dare to ask the Holy Spirit to empower you today?

The more we become in tune with God and enlivened in our Christian faith, the better we can connect with other people and share the gospel with them. What could be more attractive than the fruit of the Spirit made evident in our lives: love, joy, peace, patience, kindness, goodness, faithfulness, gentleness and self-control (Galatians 5:22–23)?

Part of our witness is in the way we deal with the inevitable problems of life in our relationship with God. We all have them: the question is whether we let them get in the way. It is very easy to think, 'If I was a better Christian, I would be a better witness.' You will do nothing if you think like that. Issues may not go away but they need not be a stumbling-block either to our own growth in God or to other people finding faith in Jesus.

Sharing faith comes out of our experience and relationship with the Lord. As we work through our difficulties, we may find that others are drawn to faith as a result. Earlier, I mentioned Mark. Blind since birth, he is now the leader of a worship band. He makes some interesting points about his relationship with God in this respect:

Blindness can be physical, spiritual or intellectual. 'Amazing grace' is a powerful song as the first three verses are about grace. I have experienced that in my life. For me, 'I once was blind but now I see' is about light and darkness. Blindness itself is not a problem. I think of John's Gospel and the notion that light shines in darkness and darkness did not understand it. As a blind person I think of it as 'presence and void'. You could read John 1:5 as 'Presence gives shape to the void and the void cannot overwhelm it', for example.

Mark is very ready to engage other people in discussion about these issues, which flow out of his relationship with God.

A young woman called Lynda is another example of someone who came to faith through difficulties. She went deaf as a young mother and, later on, her husband died. With the help and support of Christians, she took many steps in faith and is now training to be a church minister, thus helping other people come to faith too. She looks back on her faith journey and says, 'God allowed me to become deaf for a reason.' In Chapter 4 we noted that 20 per cent of new Christians said 'bereavement' had been one of the reasons they had came to faith. Those people are often the ones who have a ministry of helping other bereaved people find faith too—a ministry that grows out of their experience and relationship with Jesus.

Facing challenges is part of the Jesus way: the Lord experienced rejection and even crucifixion, and stands with us in any problems we face. Although some evangelists like to present faith in God as a way of making life easy, the challenges are part of the whole gospel picture. 'Good news' is not about avoiding difficulties but about finding the help of the Holy Spirit as we work through those problems. This is important for its own sake, but it is also part of our witness to other people who are interested in our faith journey and who look to us to tell them more.

So we come back to the Holy Spirit and your relationship with God, overflowing to other people and enabling you to be a witness. Here are a few ways in which he has prompted people like you and me in the past; let me encourage you to pray for opportunities in the future.

- **Words:** From that first encounter with the bully in the playground, when I felt that God gave me the words to say, to the many times in my recent experience when I've thought 'Where did that come from?' I know that God's Holy Spirit gives us the words. My experience is also that people who do not go to church are often more ready to hear about Jesus than we are to speak of him. Have a go! Ask a question, start a conversation, be open to what the other person says, have a stimulating debate and leave it to be continued.
- **Actions:** How often have you been prompted to do something, and only afterwards discovered the reason for your action? The possibilities range from picking up the phone to a friend or going to their house with a cake or pot plant, to inviting someone to stay or taking an ongoing responsibility like becoming a school governor or joining a church ministry team. Pray for the Spirit's guidance in everything you do, be relaxed, trust in God to guide you, and respond to what's going on around you.
- **Prayer:** We have thought about praying for people and how it is usually an encouragement. Spending time in prayer is a great gift, and the more we pray, the more God's work is done. We pray, 'Your kingdom come, your will be done on earth as it is in heaven; (Matthew 6:10), being open to what the answer to that prayer might be. We should remember, too, that we can pray with the authority

of Jesus' name (John 14:14). Drop somebody a note, send a text, or leave a Facebook message to let people know that you are thinking and praying for them.

- **Miracles**: My own view is that we see lots of miracles every day but they usually go unnoticed because we tend to look for one big miracle that sorts out all our problems in one go. Pray in faith about the small things in life and be thankful for small blessings, seeing each one as evidence that God is at work in our lives and in the lives of the people we seek to serve. Miracles were part of the Jesus way: they still are today.

- **Guidance**: Many of us ask daily for the Spirit to guide us. We have to trust that our prayer will be answered in God's way. Ordinary circumstances can become extraordinary events if we are open to letting God use us. Guidance— just like the other blessings listed above—comes as we remain open and ask for the Holy Spirit. Pray for the people you seek to reach with good news, that they will know this guidance for themselves.

Of course, even though we rely on the Holy Spirit, we can still get things wrong. Billy Graham, one of the greatest evangelists of all time, tells how, in the early days of his ministry, he got lost trying to find the large stadium where he was going to speak. He pulled over in his car and asked a passer-by for help. The man gave Billy directions and showed him the way. At the close of the conversation, Billy thought he'd take the opportunity to share his faith. Since they had talked about directions, Billy said, 'I'll be giving people directions to heaven tonight. Would you like to come and hear them?' The man replied, 'You must be joking. Do you really expect me to listen to you giving me directions to heaven when you can't even find your way around earth?' [62]

At the end of the day, we are simply called to follow Jesus, live as Christians and do what we normally do—and do it well. We can work through the difficulties in life as a witness to God's faithfulness. We can look to Jesus, the 'author and perfecter of our faith' (Hebrews 12:2), and rely on the Holy Spirit as well as our own gifts and abilities. Let God use your personality and the networks you already have. Feed your faith by prayer, Bible reading and fellowship, and trust that your faith will flow over to other people. I think again of the quotation I mentioned in the introduction to this book: 'Success in witnessing is simply presenting Jesus Christ, in the power of the Holy Spirit, and leaving the results to God.'

'Follow-up activities

If you are feeling 'dry' in your faith and feel that you have nothing to share, don't despair. Refresh your faith with one of these activities.

- Take five minutes to record the activities of a typical day. Where is there space for you to spend time with God?
- Talk to a friend and pray together about the pattern of life you lead.
- If you don't already do so, start using daily Bible reading notes, such as those published by BRF.
- Join *Foundations21* [63] to explore many aspects of Christian discipleship in greater depth.

- Go on a Quiet Day or longer retreat.
- Read a Christian classic book such as *The Imitation of Christ* by Thomas à Kempis or *The Practice of the Presence of God* by Brother Lawrence.
- Take up a challenge that will stretch you, such as raising money for a Christian charity or visiting another part of the world in a cultural exchange.
- Join in with some outreach activity through your local network of churches, such as a faith-sharing team or project group.
- Explore options for finding a mentor or spiritual director who can help you develop your spiritual life.
- Find a small group or prayer partner to pray with regularly. (They don't have to be members of your own church!)

Working with paradox

'The greatest among you will be your servant. For whoever exalts himself will be humbled, and whoever humbles himself will be exalted.'

MATTHEW 23:11–12

As wheels in a complicated machine may move in opposite directions and yet subserve one common end, so may truths (of scripture) apparently opposite be perfectly reconcilable with each other, and equally subserve the purposes of God in the accomplishment of our salvation.[64]

CHARLES SIMEON

You might think 'Working with paradox' is a strange section title to find near the end of a book about sharing faith. I'd like to explain how I have found it helpful in sharing the gospel and leave it as another tool in the box for you to consider.

As we have considered sharing faith the Jesus way, we have looked at the gospel message from the perspective of the many different things Jesus said to people in his day. The list of Top Fifty texts in Appendix A provides us with a big picture—but one that includes apparent opposites. Here is a striking example:

'For whoever is not against us is for us' (Mark 9:40).
'He who is not with me is against me' (Matthew 12:30; Luke 11:23).

We have seen that there are various aspects to the gospel message and Jesus addressed each individual with his or her own tailor-made message. For example, he gave two different answers to the question, 'What must I do to inherit eternal life?' In the scriptures and in our experience, there is a creative tension. We have to hold different ideas together at the same time. I have found that many people who do not call themselves Christians understand this readily—sometimes more readily than those who have been Christians for a long time. Talking about opposites, creative tension, paradox and the 360 gospel has often engaged people in conversation to the extent that they end up saying, 'We must talk a lot more about that again.' In the process, we are touching on many different aspects of the gospel and finding points of connection and follow-up.

A simple definition of paradox is 'opposites that co-exist

at the same time and with tension in between'. Many things are not 'pure' paradox but they illustrate the principle. When I say, 'It's amazing: Jesus was born of a virgin mother', that's paradoxical, fascinating and a potential conversation starter. In the same way, we can think of Jesus being both God and man, or the 'Alpha and Omega': these ideas make people think a bit more deeply about the gospel.

In a previous study,[65] I found that there were 26 examples of the principle of paradox in Matthew's Gospel. Matthew 23:11–12 (quoted at the beginning of this section) is one example, and here is another: 'Whoever wants to save his life will lose it, but whoever loses his life for me will find it' (Matthew 16:25). Quoting a text like that makes people think and provides an opportunity for discussion. It engages the brain, prompting the question, 'What do you think Jesus means by this?'

Paradox in the gospel can also help us connect the words of Jesus with experience, for both ourselves and the people for whom we pray. In our own lives we recognise paradox as tension between opposites, often between what we believe and what we actually do. The apostle Paul understood this: he records how he pleaded with the Lord to remove a 'thorn in his flesh', eventually coming to the conclusion that 'when I am weak, then I am strong' (2 Corinthians 12:7–10). Sometimes, in evangelism, it is helpful to admit that we Christians have problems too, and we face them with God's help. This is not only a witness to an authentic faith, but it makes us appear less superior and more understanding of the issues other people face.

Those whom we seek to reach with the good news live

complex lives. Sometimes, what they need most is a simple message to help them start to make sense of life, and to them Jesus says, 'Follow me'. At other times, they need to know that the gospel connects with all the complex issues they face. This is when they need to know that there are as many facets to Jesus as there are to their problems. Jesus experienced both the horrors of crucifixion and the glory of resurrection. There is nothing we experience today that he does not connect with, have sympathy for or understand to the full, and that he wishes to redeem. Remember the parable of the loving father who knew about letting go, loss, family tensions, greed, trust, failure, hope, restoration and encouragement (Luke 15:11–32)? Jesus understands every facet and every source of tension in life—which is good news for people who struggle.

The principle of paradox also helps us in our own relationship with God and understanding of faith. James Fowler is a developmental psychologist who has applied the stages of life to faith journeys and writes about the way our faith becomes more complex as we grow in Christ. He uses the analogy of the way a child becomes an adult, and the various stages of development that can be observed at different ages. Talking about 'faith development' theory, he says, 'One who becomes a Christian in childhood may indeed remain Christian all of his or her life. But one's way of being Christian will need to deepen, expand, and be reconstituted several times in the pilgrimage of faith.'[66] Fowler's 'fifth stage' focuses on being able to cope with paradox in the Christian faith. It is often not a case of 'either / or' but 'both / and' when we look at Jesus.

Have another look at the Top 50 texts and see if you can find any examples of opposites, tension or paradox.

In my conversations with people about the Christian faith, I have often found the principle of paradox enlivening. It provides an opportunity to listen to them and understand the tensions they face, it gives a chance to quote different aspects of the gospel, and it leaves the opportunity to continue the conversation another time. Strangely, I have also found it helpful when talking to people who have been committed Christians for a long time and have a lot of questions and issues to face. In some cases, it helps them to hold issues in tension and keeps them from giving up on God altogether.

The word 'paradox' is not commonly used by most people, and sometimes it is best avoided. It may be easier to use the image of the diamond and speak about the many facets of the gospel, which again may connect with the experience of the other person. Sometimes I'll use the image of a jigsaw, a big picture made up of small pieces of the various gospel texts. However we look at it, as in everything else, we look to Jesus as the one whom we want people to come to know and love.

Follow-up activities

- Consider any opposites and tensions you are aware of—in your own life or the lives of your friends and acquaintances. Pray that we may all find Jesus and the gospel relevant.

- Discuss the principle of paradox with a friend and consider the implications of the fact that Jesus said different things to different people, sometimes appearing contradictory. Does the concept of paradox open doors for conversations with people who would not call themselves Christians?
- If you are in a discussion group, here are some 'opposites in creative tension'. Can you add to the list?

  - ❖ Born of a virgin mother
  - ❖ Jesus as both God and man
  - ❖ The lion and the lamb
  - ❖ The servant king
  - ❖ Alpha and Omega, the beginning and the end

- Finally, if you are in a group, have a discussion about this book and what has been most helpful in equipping you to share faith the Jesus way. Pray and plan what to do next. If you have a story to share with other groups, email me at jim.currin@jesus360.org.uk.
- If you are a church leader, are there aspects of this book that have been particularly useful? Review how you might help people in your church to share their faith in Jesus Christ. Here is a mini-audit of questions for you and your leadership team to consider:

  - ❖ If you have not been doing so, could you have a six-week series of sermons or discussion groups, or a short course on sharing faith? See Appendix C for a basic outline suggestion.
  - ❖ Is there a way of coaching and mentoring the people who want to do more in the way of evangelism?
  - ❖ Do you and your leadership team have a strategic plan for mission and evangelism?

❖ Are there resources or projects you can encourage people to get involved in, which would be the natural next step in their faith journey?

❖ Are there mission initiatives, either local or national, that could help you and other congregations nearby to share the good news of Jesus Christ together?

Moving with the wind of the Spirit

'Come, follow me,' Jesus said.
MATTHEW 4:19

'You will receive power when the Holy Spirit comes on you; and you will be my witnesses in Jerusalem, and in all Judea and Samaria, and to the ends of the earth.'
ACTS 1:8

In *Sharing Faith the Jesus Way*, I have offered you several images. There is the triangle of two-way relationships as a guide to what goes on when we help other people find faith in Jesus. There is the many-faceted diamond, which speaks of the way individuals might see a particular aspect of the gospel that speaks to their need. At the conclusion of this book, I'd like to add one more image, to illustrate the adventure I have been on as a Christian and to encourage you as we move forward together as disciples.

The picture is of a sailing boat slicing through the water. To get anywhere in this boat, you harness the wind by continually adjusting and balancing five different and equally essential controls at the same time. In a modern racing dinghy, this means adjusting the sails, the centreboard, the rudder, and the position where you sit on the boat (there are two elements to this: front to back and side to side). Your movements have to be precise because you are bringing a complex set of opposing forces together. Anything less than this balance acts as a brake. The more finely balanced you are, the faster you travel.

Of course, Peter's fishing boat was different from a modern sailing dinghy, but I suspect he, and even Jesus, would have experienced some of the same essentials that make a boat move.

The logo for Churches Together is a sailing boat. We are being blown by the wind of the Spirit, and the church is the boat from which we fish. Note, however, that this boat is not a battleship, not a life raft and not a cruise ship either. It is a humble fishing boat, because, whether we act as individuals or as a church fellowship, our task is to make 'fishers of men'. 'Follow me,' says Jesus, 'and see how it is to be done.' He spent three years training his followers on the job. All they had to do was to bring people to Jesus, and he would do the rest. Essentially this is still all we need to do today.

Appendix A

Top 50 texts for the 360 gospel of Jesus

Here is a list of 50 things Jesus said to different people at different times in the four Gospels. Some are similar to others and some are very different. The criterion for my choice was that each could be an answer to the question, 'What must I do to inherit eternal life?' The italics are all mine, to make the point of what we should do, be or become.

There is an old saying: 'A text out of context is a pretext'. Providing a list like this one raises lots of questions, some of which I have explored in *The 360 Gospel of Jesus*, which I have written about on the website to accompany this book: www. jesus360.org.uk.

1. *Repent and believe* the good news (Mark 1:15).
2. *Follow me* (Matthew 4:19).
3. Blessed are the *poor in spirit*, for theirs is the kingdom of heaven (Matthew 5:3) (or 'Blessed are you who are poor' in Luke 6:20).
4. Blessed are those who *hunger and thirst for righteousness*, for they will be filled (Matthew 5:6).
5. Blessed are the *pure in heart*, for they will see God (Matthew 5:8).

6. Blessed are the *peacemakers*, for they will be called children of God (Matthew 5:9, NRSV).

7. Blessed are those who are *persecuted for righteousness' sake*, for theirs is the kingdom of heaven (Matthew 5:10, NRSV).

8. Beware of practising your piety before others in order to be seen by them… *Your Father who sees in secret will reward you* (Matthew 6:1, 4, NRSV).

9. *Strive first for the kingdom of God and his righteousness*, and all these things will be given to you as well (Matthew 6:33, NRSV).

10. *Do not judge, and you will not be judged*. Do not condemn, and you will not be condemned. Forgive, and you will be forgiven. Give, and it will be given to you (Luke 6:37–38).

11. *Ask, and it will be given to you*; search, and you will find; knock, and the door will be opened for you. For everyone who asks receives, and everyone who searches finds, and for everyone who knocks, the door will be opened (Matthew 7:7–8; Luke 11:9–10, NRSV).

12. Son, your *sins are forgiven* (Mark 2:5).

13. The one who *endures to the end will be saved* (Matthew 10:22; 24:13, NRSV).

14. If any want to become my followers, let them *deny themselves and take up their cross and follow me*. For those who want to save their life will lose it, and those who lose their life for my sake will find it (Matthew 16:24–25, NRSV).

15. *Come to me, all you who are weary and burdened*, and I will give you rest. Take my yoke upon you and learn from me,

for I am gentle and humble in heart, and you will find rest for your souls. For my yoke is easy and my burden is light (Matthew 11:28–30).

16. *Love your enemies, do good*, and lend, expecting nothing in return. Your reward will be great, and you will be children of the Most High. (Luke 6:35, NRSV).

17. Truly I tell you, unless you change and *become like children*, you will never enter the kingdom of heaven. Whoever becomes humble like this child is the greatest in the kingdom of heaven (Matthew 18:3–4, NRSV).

18. Whoever is not against us is for us. For truly I tell you, *whoever gives you a cup of water* to drink because you bear the name of Christ will by no means lose the reward (Mark 9:40–41, NRSV).

19. No one who *puts a hand to the plough* and looks back is fit for the kingdom of God (Luke 9:62, NRSV).

20. *Whoever is not with me is against me*, and whoever does not gather with me scatters (Matthew 12:30, NRSV).

21. Someone asked him, 'Lord, will only a few be saved? He said to them, '*Strive to enter through the narrow door*; for many, I tell you, will try to enter and will not be able' (Luke 13:23–24, NRSV).

22. When you give a banquet, *invite the poor*, the crippled, the lame, and the blind. And you will be blessed, because they cannot repay you, for you will be repaid at the resurrection of the righteous (Luke 14:13–14, NRSV).

23. 'Good Teacher, what must I do to inherit eternal life?' Jesus said to him, 'Why do you call me good? No one is good but God alone. You know the commandments: "You shall not murder; You shall not commit adultery;

You shall not steal; You shall not bear false witness; You shall not defraud; Honour your father and mother".' He said to him, 'Teacher I have kept all these since my youth.' Jesus, looking at him, loved him and said, 'You lack one thing; go, *sell what you own, and give the money to the poor, and you will have treasure in heaven; then come, follow me*' (Mark 10:17–21, NRSV).

24. To sit at my right hand and at my left, this is not mine to grant, but it is for those for whom it has *been prepared by my Father* (Matthew 20:23, NRSV).

25. For many are called, but few are chosen (Matthew 22:14, NRSV).

26. 'Teacher' he said, 'what must I do to inherit eternal life?' He said to him, 'What is written in the law? What do you read there?' He answered, '*You shall love the Lord your God with all your heart, and with all your soul, and with all your strength, and with all your mind; and your neighbour as yourself.*' And he said to him, 'You have given the right answer; do this, and you will live' (Luke 10:25–28, NRSV).

27. Then he will say to those on his left hand, 'You that are accursed, depart from me into the eternal fire prepared for the devil and his angels; for *I was hungry and you gave me no food, I was thirsty and you gave me nothing to drink, I was a stranger and you did not welcome me, naked and you did not give me clothing, sick and in prison and you did not visit me.*' Then they also will answer, 'Lord, when was it that we saw you hungry or thirsty or a stranger or naked or sick or in prison, and did not take care of you?' Then he will answer them, 'Truly I tell you, just as you did not

do it to one of the least of these, you did not do it to me.' And these will go away into eternal punishment, but the righteous into eternal life (Matthew 25:41–46, NRSV).

28. *'Jesus, remember me when you come into your kingdom.'* He replied, 'Truly I tell you, today you will be with me in Paradise' (Luke 23:42–43, NRSV).

29. *Those who love me will keep my word*, and my Father will love them, and we will come to them and make our home with them (John 14:23b, NRSV).

30. I tell you the truth, no one can enter the kingdom of God unless he is *born of water and the Spirit*. (John 3:5).

31. Whoever *believes in him* shall not perish but have eternal life (John 3:16).

32. *Whoever drinks the water I give him will never thirst*. Indeed, the water I give him will become in him a spring of water welling up to eternal life (John 4:14).

33. Do not be amazed at this, for a time is coming when all who are in their graves will hear his voice and come out—*those who have done good will rise to live*, and those who have done evil will rise to be condemned (John 5:28–29).

34. Do not work for food that spoils, but for food that endures to eternal life, which the Son of Man will give you (John 6:27).

35. 'What must we do to do the works God requires?' Jesus answered, 'The work of God is this: to *believe in the one he has sent*' (John 6:28–29).

36. I am the bread of life. He who comes to me will never go hungry, and *he who believes in me will never be thirsty* (John 6:35).

37. For my Father's will is that *everyone who looks to the Son and believes in him shall have eternal life*, and I will raise him up at the last day (John 6:40).

38. No one can *come to me* unless the Father who sent me draws him, and I will raise him up at the last day (John 6:44).

39. *Whoever eats my flesh and drinks my blood has eternal life*, and I will raise him up at the last day (John 6:54).

40. I am the light of the world. *Whoever follows me will never walk in darkness*, but will have the light of life (John 8:12).

41. I told you that you would die in your sins; if you do not *believe that I am the one I claim to be*, you will indeed die in your sins (John 8:24).

42. *If you hold to my teaching, you are really my disciples*. Then you will know the truth, and the truth will set you free (John 8:31–32).

43. I tell you the truth, everyone who sins is a slave to sin… *So if the Son sets you free, you will be free indeed* (John 8:34, 36).

44. I am the gate; *whoever enters through me will be saved* (John 10:9).

45. *My sheep listen to my voice; I know them, and they follow me*. I give them eternal life, and they shall never perish (John 10:27–28).

46. I am the resurrection and the life. *He who believes in me will live*, even though he dies; and whoever lives and believes in me will never die (John 11:25–26).

47. *The man who loves his life will lose it, while the man who hates his life in this world will keep it* for eternal life (John 12:25).

48. I am the way and the truth and the life. *No one comes to the Father except through me* (John 14:6).
49. *If anyone loves me, he will obey my teaching.* My Father will love him, and we will come to him and make our home with him (John 14:23).
50. Now this is eternal life: that they may *know you, the only true God, and Jesus Christ, whom you have sent* (John 17:3).

Which of these texts have been the most significant for you? A questionnaire based on this list asked people in different congregations which text resonated most with (a) their initial understanding of faith in the past, (b) their faith as it is in the present, and (c) their hope for the future. I have used the questionnaire in a number of places and you could use it in your small group or congregation. Of course, there are many more relevant Bible texts outside the four Gospels, but this has proved an interesting exercise none the less. See www. jesus360.org.uk for more information.

Appendix B

Resources

Resources referred to in the text are listed in the endnotes.

- **Jesus 360 website:** Supporting *Sharing Faith the Jesus Way* and *The 360 Gospel of Jesus* with information, resources, articles and links to a blog site for readers' comments and contributions: www.jesus360.org.uk
- **Evangelism UK:** a news service that provides headlines and web links by email, free to subscribers at www. evangelismuk.typepad.com.
- **Churches Together in England website:** information and resources for evangelism in England to help churches work together in sharing the good news of Jesus Christ: www.cte.org.uk/evangelisation

Particular resources linked to this study include the following.

Websites

- **www.rejesus.co.uk** is a website about Jesus for people who do not go to church.
- **www.christianity.org.uk** explores many aspects of the Christian faith for people who want to find out more.

- **www.biblefresh.com** is a national initiative in 2011 and beyond to encourage people in church and the wider society to engage with the biblical text for the 400th anniversary of the King James Version.
- **www.foundations21.org.uk** is a free online study resource designed for Christians who want to explore twelve major aspects of Christian discipleship.
- **www.faith-journeys.com** is the *Christian Research* website from which I have quoted. It provides a place for you to write up your own faith journey and read other people's stories.
- **www.spiritualjourneys.org.uk** is a resource linked to a book called *Sense Making Faith* by Anne Richards, which explores faith journeys with Jesus through the various senses.

Biblical studies

- *Learning Evangelism from Jesus*, Jerram Barrs (Crossway, 2009). Provides an exploration of 15 key Gospel passages and the lessons we learn from each one about evangelism.
- *The Biblical Foundations for Mission*, Donald Senior and Carroll Stuhlmueller (SCM, 1983) and reprints. You will have to search for this classic volume, but it is a fantastic overview of mission throughout the Bible.
- *Sharing Faith: Biblical reflections for today*, Gavin Wakefield (BRF, 2004). A collection of short reflections about mission from different parts of the Old and New Testament.
- *The Four Gospels and the One Gospel of Jesus Christ*, Martin Hengel (SCM, 2000). This is a technical analysis using the

historical-critical method of the four Gospels and shows how we derive the gospel we share today.

- *Jesus through Middle Eastern Eyes*, Kenneth E. Bailey (SPCK, 2008). This book illuminates Gospel passages and Jesus' encounters with people, by analysing the cultural context of Jesus' day.
- *Blind Spots in the Bible*, Adrian Plass (BRF, 2006). Explores a wide range of Bible passages that are 'puzzles and paradoxes that we tend to avoid'.

Evangelism

- *Jesus the Evangelist*, Robin Gamble (David Cook, 2009). A very helpful book showing how Jesus was an evangelist and why we should learn evangelism the Jesus way.
- Grove Books Evangelism series (see www.grovebooks. co.uk). The following titles have informed this book: *Mission Accompaniment* (Ev 69), *Paradox in the Gospel?* (Ev 74), *Conversion Today* (Ev 75), *Telling our Faith Story* (Ev 85) and *The 360 Gospel of Jesus* (2011).
- *Breaking the News: Sharing faith without fear*, J John (Authentic, 2009). Looks at the three stories—his story, your story and their story.
- *The Art of Connecting*, Roy Crowne and Bill Muir with Angela Little (Authentic, 2003). Another look at the three stories mentioned above, in the context of young people sharing their faith.
- *More Ways than One: Evangelism in a postmodern world*, J John et al. (Authentic, 2009). Various contributors de-

scribe how they approach evangelism through comedy, singing, preaching and storytelling.
- *Gone but Not Forgotten* (DLT, 1998), and the follow-up resource book *Gone for Good?* (Epworth, 2007) by Philip Richter and Leslie J. Francis. Exploring recent research over a ten-year period about church leaving and returning.

Further resources relating to the material in this book will be posted on www.jesus360.org.uk.

Appendix C

Summary questions for a six-week series

Here are the main Bible passages and summary key questions:

Week 1: Jesus accepts you as you are
(Chapter 1 and 'Your story')

The woman at the well: John 4:4–26
- How did Jesus accept the woman as she was?
- What was the conversation they had in the heat of the day?
- What was the outcome of Jesus' accepting this outcast?

Week 2: Jesus respects the other person and sees their need
(Chapter 2 and 'Their story')

The man through the roof: Luke 5:17–26
- For what need was the man brought to Jesus?
- What need(s) did Jesus meet?
- What was the outcome of this encounter?

Week 3: God's love is the key to the gospel
(Chapter 3 and 'God's story')

The parable of the lost son or loving father: Luke 15:11–32
- How did the father demonstrate his love for the younger son?
- What do we learn from the attitude of the father and both sons?
- What does this say about God's love for us?

Week 4: Prayer, care, and share the good news
(Chapter 4 and 'Communication between 'you' and 'them'')

The expert in the law asks about eternal life: Luke 10:25–37
- What answer did Jesus give to the lawyer's question?
- What was the lawyer's question?
- What does this say about the different facets of the gospel?

Week 5: Accompany those who follow Jesus
(Chapter 5 and 'Their' response to 'God')

The call of the fishermen: Matthew 4:18–22; 5:1–16
- How did Jesus call and what did he say the fishermen were to do?
- How did Jesus accompany his followers?
- What did the disciples do with what they learnt from the master?

Week 6: Your journey: going on with God
(Chapter 6 and 'You' in your relationship with 'God')

Jesus reinstatement of Peter: John 21:15–19
- How is the faith journey story of Peter like ours?
- What was the attitude of Jesus to Peter's denial?
- What did the Holy Spirit empower Peter to do next?

Sermon notes and discussion material based on *Sharing Faith the Jesus Way* are to be found on www.jesus360.org.uk.

✛

Notes

1 John V. Taylor, *Mission as Dialogue*, quoted in *Pray Every Day*, ed. Ronald Jasper (Collins, 1976), p. 51 (with 'man' changed to 'person' in the last sentence).

2 www.faith-journeys.com.

3 www.christian-research.org.uk.

4 At the Forum of Churches Together in England, 7–9 September 2009.

5 Paul Heelas and Linda Woodhead, *The Spiritual Revolution* (Blackwell, 2005).

6 Statistics and comment from Steven Croft et al., *Evangelism in a Spiritual Age* (CHP, 2005) pp. 9–10.

7 The point is well made in Pope Benedict XVI, *Jesus of Nazareth* (Bloomsbury, 2007) p. xii, and is explored by Tom Wright, *The Challenge of Jesus* (SPCK, 2000). Other people writing and speaking about recovering the 'Jesus way' are Tony Campolo, Brian McLaren and Steve Chalke.

8 Quoted by Bob Mayo in *Gospel Exploded* (Triangle, 1996), p. 12.

9 For information about Church Army work, visit www.churcharmy.co.uk.

10 Sadhu Sundar Singh, quoted in *40 Days of Yes* (CMS, 2010), Day 5.

11 Nick Baines, *Jesus and People Like Us* (St Andrews Press, 2004), p. 11.

12 www.adherents.com/Religions_By_Adherents.html

13 Bill Hybels, *Becoming a Contagious Christian* (Zondervan, 1995), p. 18.

14 Philip Jinadu and David Lawrence, *Winning Ways* (Authentic, 2007), p. 11.

15 Joseph Aldrich, *The Logic of Evangelism* (Marshalls, 1981), p. 89.

16 Pope Benedict XVI, *Jesus of Nazareth*, p. xii.

17 Max Lucado, *3:16 The Numbers of Hope* (Thomas Nelson, 2007), p. xv.

18 Ruth Adams and Jan Harney, *Unlocking the Door* (Authentic / Activate, 2005), p. 24.

19 http://trevinwax.com/2008/09/04/gospel-definitions-nt-wright/

20 Hybels, *Becoming a Contagious Christian*, pp. 30, 203.

21   Hybels, *Becoming a Contagious Christian*, pp. 30, 203.

22   Hugh T. Kerr and John M. Mulder, *Conversions* (Hodder & Stoughton, 1983), pp. 15, 16.

23   Quoted in Billy Graham et al., *The Calling of an Evangelist* (World Wide Publications, 1987), p. 133.

24   Robin Gamble, *Jesus the Evangelist* (David Cook, 2009), p. 17.

25   Gamble, *Jesus the Evangelist*, pp. 66–67.

26   www.lausanne.org/about.html

27   Quoted in Jeffrey John (ed.), *Living Evangelism* (DLT, 1996), p. 9.

28   Quoted by Jerram Barrs, *Learning Evangelism from Jesus* (Crossway, 2009), p. 62.

29   Donald Senior and Carroll Stuhlmueller, *The Biblical Foundations for Mission* (SCM,1983), p. 3.

30   A good resource book for this is Janice Price, *Telling My Faith Story* (Grove Books Ev 85, 2009), www.grovebooks.co.uk.

31   *Inspire* (CPO, September 2008)

32   Found in *The Lion Christian Poetry Collection* compiled by Mary Batchelor (Lion, 1995), p. 97.

33   Billy Graham in *The Calling of an Evangelist*, p. 131.

34   Mike Springer and Kevin Higham, *Blowing Your Cover: Leader's Guide* (Monarch, 2006), p. 11.

35   www.gdoplondon.com

36   www.sttoms.net

37   Quoted in Croft et al., *Evangelism in a Spiritual Age*, p. 11.

38   See www.sharetheguide.org for examples

39   ORB survey 2003, quoted by Steve Hollinghurst in *Mission-Shaped Evangelism* (Canterbury Press, 2010), p. 194.

40   www.nationalchurchestrust.org/churches.html.

41   www.backtochurch.co.uk.

42   Search for the report pdf on www.tearfund.org.

43   http://uk.alpha.org and www.christianityexplored.org.

44   www.philotrust.com.

45   Peter Howell-Jones and Nick Wills, *Pints of View: Encounters Down the Pub* (Grove Books Ev72, 2005).

46   www.cafechurch.net.

47 Yvonne Richmond and Nick Spencer, *Beyond the Fringe* (LICC/Cliff College, 2005), p. 17.
48 Facebook group SUCU and Text a Toastie, where the questions are available on public view.
49 www.biblesociety.org.uk/reelissues and www.lyfe.org.uk.
50 See www.jesus360.org.uk.
51 Taylor, *Mission as Dialogue*, quoted in Jasper (ed.), *Pray Every Day*, p. 51 with 'man' changed to 'person' in the last sentence.
52 Bob Hopkins and Freddy Hedley, *Coaching for Missional Leadership* (ACPI, 2008), p. 33.
53 Based on the original Engel scale described in James Engel, *What's Gone Wrong with the Harvest?* (Zondervan, 1975), p. 45.
54 Laurence Singlehurst, *Sowing Reaping Keeping* (IVP, 2006).
55 www.nowachristian.org
56 Don Everts and Doug Shaupp, *Pathway to Jesus* (IVP, 2009).
57 Everts and Shaupp, *Pathway to Jesus*, p. 22.
58 John Finney, *Finding Faith Today* (Bible Society, 1992)
59 Gamble, *Jesus the Evangelist*, p. 66.
60 Pope Benedict XVI, *Jesus of Nazareth*, p. xxiv.
61 Stephen Cottrell, *Come and See* (BRF, 2011), p. 111.
62 Retold by Roy Todd in *Confident Communicator* (Kevin Mayhew, 2008), p. 44.
63 www.foundations21.org.uk is an online resource from BRF. It covers twelve aspects of discipleship, with a choice of learning styles based on the characteristics of the four Gospels.
64 Charles Simeon's preface to *Horae Homolecticae*, quoted in Handley C.G. Moule, *Charles Simeon: Biography of a Sane Saint* (IVP, 1965), p. 79, and Christopher Cocksworth, *Holding Together* (Canterbury Press, 2008), p. xi.
65 Jim Currin, *Paradox in the Gospel?* www.grovebooks.co.uk
66 Quoted in Jeff Astley, ed., *How Faith Grows* (CHP, 1994), p. 2.

❖

Further information

Jim Currin is a commissioned Church Army evangelist and currently serves as Secretary for Evangelisation at Churches Together in England.

Church Army

The Church Army is a society of evangelists in the Church of England, founded in 1882 by Wilson Carlile. Its aim is to share the good news of Jesus 'through words and action'. Today, there are around 300 CA evangelists engaged in a wide variety of evangelistic work.

See www.churcharmy.org.uk.

Churches Together in England

Churches Together in England was established in 1990 along with Cytun (Wales) and ACTS (Scotland) to offer 'resourced space' for sharing between the churches in seeking to work together. At a national level there are 31 member churches. Across England there are 2500 local 'Churches Together' groups and over 800 Local Ecumenical Partnerships of various kinds.

See www.cte.org.uk.

The Churches Group for Evangelisation

The Churches Group for Evangelisation is one of the co-ordinating groups at Churches Together in England. It brings together the national denominational evangelism officers, along with some key representatives of home mission agencies. The aim of the Churches Group for Evangelisation is 'Sharing the good news of Jesus Christ together'.

Information about the group, together with resource papers produced by it, can be seen at www.cte.org.uk/evangelisation.

Network News service

The Churches group for Evangelisation provides a news headline service for the wider network, so that the 'right hand knows what the left is doing'. Over 1000 items of interest have been posted. To see the news, archive, and place to subscribe free, visit www.evangelismuk.typepad.com.

Come and See

Learning from the life of Peter

Stephen Cottrell

When we look at the life of Peter—fisherman, disciple, leader of the Church—we find somebody who responded wholeheartedly to the call to 'come and see'. Come and meet Jesus, come and follow him, come and find your life being transformed. This book focuses on Peter, not because he is the best-known of Jesus' friends, nor the most loyal, but because he shows us what being a disciple of Jesus is actually like. Like us, he takes a step of faith and then flounders, and needs the saving touch of God to continue becoming the person he was created to be.

Come and See, first published as *On This Rock*, is also designed to help you begin to develop a pattern of Bible reading, reflection and prayer. Twenty-eight readings offer short passages from the story of Peter, plus comment and questions for personal response or group discussion.

ISBN 978 1 84101 843 0   £6.99
Available from your local Christian bookshop or, in case of diffi-culty, direct from BRF using the order form opposite. You may also order from www.brfonline.org.uk.

ORDERFORM

REF	TITLE	PRICE	QTY	TOTAL
843 0	Come and See	£6.99		

POSTAGE AND PACKING CHARGES				
Order value	UK	Europe	Surface	Air Mail
£7.00 & under	£1.25	£3.00	£3.50	£5.50
£7.01–£30.00	£2.25	£5.50	£6.50	£10.00
Over £30.00	FREE	prices on request		

Postage and packing	
Donation	
TOTAL	

Name _____ Account Number _____

Address _____

_____ Postcode _____

Telephone Number_____

Email _____

Payment by: ❏ Cheque ❏ Mastercard ❏ Visa ❏ Postal Order ❏ Maestro

Card no ☐☐☐☐ ☐☐☐☐ ☐☐☐☐ ☐☐☐☐ ▨▨▨

Valid from ☐☐☐☐ Expires ☐☐☐☐ Issue no. ▨▨▨

Security code* ☐☐☐   *Last 3 digits on the reverse of the card.   Shaded boxes for
ESSENTIAL IN ORDER TO PROCESS YOUR ORDER   Maestro use only

Signature _____ Date _____

All orders must be accompanied by the appropriate payment.

Please send your completed order form to:
BRF, 15 The Chambers, Vineyard, Abingdon OX14 3FE
Tel. 01865 319700 / Fax. 01865 319701 Email: enquiries@brf.org.uk

❏ Please send me further information about BRF publications.

Available from your local Christian bookshop.   BRF is a Registered Charity

About
brf:

BRF is a registered charity and also a limited company, and has been in existence since 1922. Through all that we do—producing resources, providing training, working face-to-face with adults and children, and via the web—we work to resource individuals and church communities in their Christian discipleship through the Bible, prayer and worship.

Our Barnabas children's team works with primary schools and churches to help children under 11, and the adults who work with them, to explore Christianity creatively and to bring the Bible alive.

To find out more about BRF and its core activities and ministries, visit:

www.brf.org.uk
www.brfonline.org.uk
www.barnabasinschools.org.uk
www.barnabasinchurches.org.uk
www.messychurch.org.uk
www.foundations21.org.uk

If you have any questions about BRF
and our work, please email us at

enquiries@brf.org.uk